# NEEDY PEOPLE

*Working Successfully with Control Freaks and Approval-holics*

by

Dale J. Dwyer, Ph.D.
dalejdwyer@gmail.com

Visit my author page!
http://dalejdwyer.com

2

## Acknowledgements

Like all creative work, there are many people to thank for the inspiration for this one. First, I'd like to thank the myriad students in my leadership and human resource management classes over the years who have provided me with the spark of wondering "why?" certain people struggle so with management and leadership in organizations. You have inspired me to answer that question here, at least in part. Second, to all those who have given me feedback about the concepts presented here, as well as critique of the writing itself, thank you. I am particularly grateful to have such thoughtful people as colleagues and friends. Finally, I am indebted to my wife, Kathy Dwyer, who has "held space" while I've been thinking, agonizing, and writing this book. Without her love and support (and some fabulous ideas to make it better), this would not be the book that it was meant to be.

# TABLE OF CONTENTS

# Preface

*We have to be ourselves, however frightening and strange that self may prove to be.* —*May Sarton*

We all know them. The people who have an opinion on everything or those who don't express any opinion at all. Our coworkers and managers who have to be in charge of every project, or those for whom every decision and every action is a test of their self-worth.

These are the Control Freaks and Approval-holics of our organizations and our lives. These are the people who drive us crazy at work.

This book is written for them and for all of us who have to deal with them every day. Most importantly, it is designed to help us learn to work with people who struggle with their relationships and with trustworthiness *because* of their high needs for control and approval.

In this book you'll explore the challenges that both leaders and employees face because of high needs for control and approval. It will also provide you with tools and practical suggestions for how to develop your own

competencies in dealing with bosses, co-workers, and peers

who have these extreme needs.

Like Jung's concept of the *shadow*,[1] all persons have

unconscious attributes that they don't recognize and that hold

them back from being successful spouses and partners,

business colleagues, employees, and leaders. As a friend of

Carl Jung, Sir Laurens van der Post apparently believed in

this same duality when he wrote,

> *In a profound sense every man has two halves to his*
> *being; he is not one person so much as two persons*
> *trying to act in unison. I believe that in the heart of*
> *each human being there is something that I can only*
> *describe as a "child of darkness" who is equal and*
> *complementary to the more obvious "child of light."*[2]

This book takes you to the "dark side" of two specific

and innate needs we all have: control and approval. For

some people, unfortunately, these needs become so extreme

---

[1] Jung, C.J. (1923). *Psychological Types*. New York: Harcourt & Brace
[2] Van der Post, L. (1994). *Feather Fall: An Analogy*. Edited. by Jean-Marc Pottiez. New York: William Morrow & Company.

that they negatively affect relationships, job performance, and career success.

As leaders and members of organizations, we must deal not only with both halves of ourselves, but also with both halves of our bosses, co-workers, and peers. To do so effectively takes understanding of what makes up each half, as well as knowing how best to respond to the "light" and "dark" behaviors we all demonstrate.

## Who Should Read This Book

Everybody knows or works with someone who is over-controlling or who needs a great deal of approval. In fact, it is often the case that these are the very people who drive us crazy in the workplace! It also may be that you are dealing with your own struggles with needing control or approval. In either case, Needy People is written for you.

The insights and tools you will discover here will help you to better understand how extreme control and approval needs have influenced how we view and work with groups, teams, leaders, and co-workers, as well as how they affect job performance and career development. Needy People will also help you learn to work with bosses, peers, and direct reports who need a lot of control or who constantly engage in approval-seeking behaviors.

I hope after finishing Needy People you'll recognize how the extremes of these two needs (control and approval) prevent us from attaining the trust and credibility we must cultivate to have a meaningful connection to others, both in our workplaces and in our personal lives. But more than that, I hope that you are able to learn and apply the strategies in the book so that you may work more successfully with people who drive you crazy!

# CHAPTER 1

## Who's YOUR Chuck?

*"In my beginning is my end."*

—T.S. Eliot, from *Four Quartets: East Coker*

I want you to close your eyes and think about the person who most drives you crazy at work. This person can be a boss, a peer, or a direct report.

Got him or her pictured?

Whether it is a man or a woman, from here on we'll call your person "Chuck." Everybody has a Chuck, and everybody's Chuck is different. But I'll bet that YOUR Chuck demonstrates at least 3-5 behaviors that drive you nuts and, further, that those behaviors have their roots in high needs for control, approval, or both.

Over the past two decades, I have had the privilege of working with over 900 first-time leaders who struggled with some very common challenges. Each one created a written plan that included development of core strengths, as well as the top 3-4 challenges that they believed prevented them (or would prevent them) from becoming effective in their leadership roles. In fact, for most of their personal and professional lives they had struggled with most of the challenges they named.

As I talked with them about their challenges, I began to see patterns emerge, not just in the challenges they named, but also in the root causes they attributed to those challenges. In preparation for writing this book, each of these individual leadership development plans was reviewed in detail. The most prevalent challenges for first-time leaders (i.e., those that were mentioned more than 100 times) appear in the order in which they were mentioned most frequently:

| Most Common Challenges for New Leaders |
|---|
| 1. Lack of Emotional Control (i.e., Impatience, Anger Management, Bullying) |
| 2. Inability or Unwillingness to Delegate |
| 3. Lack of Communication Skills (i.e., Interpersonal and Fear of Public Speaking) |
| 4. Inability or Unwillingness to Deal with Conflict |
| 5. Tendency Toward Perfectionism |
| 6. Difficulty in Making Decisions |

It is also worth noting that leaders at all levels have been found to have similar issues. For example, several research studies[3] have identified the following behaviors as the primary causes for senior-level professional failure:

---

[3] See, for example, Lombardo, M.M., Ruderman, M. N., and McCauley, C.D. (1988). Explanations of success and derailment in upper-level management positions, *Journal of Business and Psychology*, 2, 3, pp.199 – 216; Dolitch, D.L. and Cairo P.C. (2003). *Why CEOs Fail*. San Francisco, CA: Jossey-Bass/John Wiley & Sons, Inc.

| Most Common Challenges for Experienced Leaders |
|---|
| 1. Had a bullying style, often viewed as intimidating, insensitive, and abrasive |
| 2. Viewed as being cold, aloof, and arrogant |
| 3. Betrayed personal trust |
| 4. Viewed as overly ambitious |
| 5. Micromanaged, unable to delegate and build a team |
| 6. Had difficulty making decisions |
| 7. Were perfectionists |

As you can see, the lists for both new and experienced leaders are very similar. Now, let's return to your Chuck.

Could THIS Be Your Chuck?

Our first Chuck is 37, a serious and rather introverted man. He is a major sports enthusiast and has played baseball and golf since he was 6 years old. Much of his self-esteem comes from the affirmation he has received over the years from his parents, teammates, and coaches, and he depends heavily on approval from others for affirmation of his talents. He has always taken his role seriously on any team of which he has been a part, and he sometimes gets upset when other players or co-workers "goof off" or try to outshine their teammates. Professionally, he is an architect, and after three successful years designing buildings with a professional architecture firm—even sharing an award with a colleague— he has recently joined a large construction firm as a Project and Design Manager, managing a team of construction workers. It's his first leadership and management role and, like his previous sports team experiences, he is taking this new role as "team manager" very seriously.

## Or Could THIS Be Your Chuck?

This Chuck is 25 and is a very petite, gregarious woman. She is a recent MBA graduate who is determined to be President and CEO of an organization by the time she's 40. She is very opinionated, but she manages to get her way much of the time because of her infectious personality. For as long as she can remember she has felt a need to be in control. A little more than a year ago, right out of college, she joined a national retail chain as a manager trainee as she worked on her graduate degree at night. In two weeks she will receive her first assignment as a store manager, replacing a manager who has just retired. She is determined to make her store the most profitable one in the region and be promoted quickly to a regional manager's position.

All of us have at least some need for approval from others and some need to control our environments. Obviously, a "Chuck" of any stripe is no different. But the configuration of approval needs and control needs will influence how "Chucks" address the major challenges they struggle with as new leaders.

In our first example, Chuck struggles with a high need for approval. In a large organization like the construction firm, he is likely to face a number of problems because of the nature of the employees he will supervise.

Because of the disparity in education level between Chuck and the construction workers, coupled with a cultural difference between what he is used to in a professional architecture firm and what he is about to experience in the blue-collar world of construction, Chuck may become impatient with his subordinates if they don't seem to take their jobs as seriously as he does. His impatient reaction may lead to assigning blame to his subordinates or to try to cover up for them in order to avoid disapproval from his boss. In order to avoid disapproval from his construction subordinates, he may avoid talking with them about his concerns with their behaviors, thereby thinking he will avoid conflict and confrontation,. As a result, Chuck may not get the affirmation he is used to receiving, either from his construction project team or from his boss. Ultimately, he may come to believe that he isn't cut out for this job and give up entirely, preferring to retreat to the security of what he has had affirmation for in the past—designing buildings.

On the other hand, our second Chuck may begin her store management assignment believing she is able to effect change in her new store simply by demanding that her subordinates do things her way. Of course, because she is personable, she initially may be able to cajole them into some changes; but, ultimately, she will probably get impatient and angry because their new behaviors may be short-lived. She is likely to become impatient with followers who have ideas different from how she thinks something "ought" to be, and may even become angry at those who challenge her way of working or her requirements that they do something a certain way. As a result, Chuck might come to believe that she is the only person who can be depended upon to get things done, resulting in a refusal to delegate work and decision-making to her subordinates. Ultimately, she may become overwhelmed by trying to do everything herself and, sadly, be seen as a distrustful, self-centered leader by her subordinates and an ineffective change agent by her boss.

For both types of "Chuck," their major challenges play out in different ways. Part of their struggle lies in how leaders and followers interact with each other and, particularly, how followers affect the ways their leaders react to them.

## Followers and Their Effect on Leaders

Robert Kelley[4] has studied followership and concludes that there are five different types of followers:

1. *Alienated Followers* are individuals who are capable, but cynical, who are troublesome, negative, and not "team players." Kelley believes that alienated followers may have been exemplary employees at one time, but became disgruntled by obstacles or setbacks in their jobs or organizations.

2. *Conformist Followers* are the "yes people" of the organization who carry out the leader's wishes

---

[4] Kelley, R. E. (1992). *The Power of Followership* (New York: Doubleday).

uncritically, particularly if that leader is strong-willed and autocratic.

3.   *Pragmatist Followers* are rarely committed to the goals of either the leader or the organization, but follow because it is politically or practically expedient for them to do so.  These followers may be indicative of a culture that avoids risks and punishes failures.

4.   *Passive Followers* allow the leader to do all the thinking for them.  They lack initiative and a sense of personal responsibility for their jobs, and they are often seen by the leader as lazy, incompetent, and unmotivated.

5.   *Exemplary Followers* are, of course, those employees who are seen by everyone as independent, innovative, self-motivated, and they apply their talents and gifts for the benefit of the organization.  They are often very adept at getting along with co-workers and leaders because they put the organization's needs ahead of their own.

In our first Chuck's case, he is likely to treat all except the Exemplary Followers as members of what Graen and Cashman[5] refer to as the out-group in their *Vertical Dyad Linkage Theory* (VDL) of leadership, also known as Leader-Member Exchange Theory or LMX. In this view, leaders influence the out-group by coercion, rewards, and invoking their legitimate authority and power as the leader. In contrast, Chuck will see the Exemplary Followers as members of his in-group, and rely on trust, added responsibility, and special treatment to influence their behavior. In previous research, in-groups have generally been shown to receive higher performance evaluations, have better relationships with each other and with the leader, and have lower levels of turnover.[6]

Treating the majority of his subordinates as out-group members will become a challenge for Chuck, because

---

[5] Graen, G. and Cashman, J.F. (1975). A Role-Making Model of Leadership in Formal Organizations: A Developmental Approach, in *Leadership Frontiers*, Ed. J.G. Hunt and L.L. Larson. Kent, OH: Kent State University Press.
[6] Liden, R. and Graen, G. (1980). Generalizability of the Vertical Dyad Linkage Model of Leadership. *Academy of Management Journal*, 23, pp. 451-465.

his short temper and demonstrated irritation with the out-group members will have a tendency to alienate him from many of his followers. As a result, he will need to learn how to control his emotions (anger and irritation, particularly) when he is interacting with them and when he is evaluating their performance.

On the other hand, the second Chuck's in-group would be made up primarily of those followers who are more passive and pragmatic. Her impatience will likely be directed to employees who act more independently and who see options and directions differently from the way she does. Her anger may stem from her inability to maintain control over their behavior and her environment, in general. Also, if she is seen as treating passive and uncritical followers more favorably than independent thinkers and "exemplary" employees, then Chuck's management decisions might also come under scrutiny from her boss and her followers.

As you can see, need for approval and need for control not only influence a leader's own behavior, but also influence the employees whom leaders see as members of their in-group and out-group. Consequently, they must be able to understand why they get irritated and angry at some followers so that they can begin to work on this challenge.

The bottom line is that control and approval are important needs that we all have. But, the people who drive you crazy at work—YOUR Chucks—usually have very high needs for control, approval, or both that affect relationships with their bosses, peers, and direct reports. So, let us begin by examining these two basic of causes for most professional and interpersonal challenges. Then, once we understand their genesis, we will discover how we might approach grappling with them.

# CHAPTER 2

## WHAT IS A CONTROL FREAK?

*The best years of your life are the ones in which you decide your problems are your own. You don't blame them on your mother, the ecology, or the President. You realize that you control your own destiny.*

–Albert Ellis, Clinical Psychologist and founder of Rational Emotive Behavioral Therapy

Control is a fundamental human and animal need; first and foremost, it is a survival tool that is used to avoid being taken advantage of by others. We likely get it from our earliest prehistoric ancestors. It is a response to go on the offensive and to take a position of strength in our environment. However, an overly controlling response occurs when relinquishing control becomes so distressing that it results in an obsession with maintaining that control— a type of obsessive-compulsive personality trait. This can result in the inability to accept new courses of action, even when it is in our best interests to do so. It also can lead to feeling overly concerned for the welfare of others to the point that they may feel impotent in dealing with their own situations and behaviors. People who are overly controlling tend to squash others' creativity, tread on individual rights and responsibilities, and generally try to create a culture of automatons. Moreover, they often lose perspective on situations.

There is an old story told by philosopher and psychologist, William James,[7] of a man who slid down a cliff on a very dark night. Obviously scared, he caught hold of a branch that stopped his fall; for hours he remained clinging to the branch, trying desperately to hold on for dear life. Gradually, he felt the strength go out of his arms, and he finally realized that his muscles just couldn't hold on any longer. With a despairing farewell to life, he let go… and dropped onto a ledge that was just six inches below him! So much of his agony could have been spared if he could have

---

[7] James, W. (1902). *The Varieties of Religious Experience*. Reproduced by Modern Library Paperback, a division of Random House, Inc. (1999).

seen his situation in the proper perspective and stopped struggling to maintain control.

Control can also be used as a defense mechanism to avoid full emotional involvement with others. A person who exerts undue self-control over his emotions hides behind an invisible shield that he believes protects him from hurt and disappointment. In reality, it prevents the emotional connection with others that is required for establishing relationships built on trust. That is, by remaining disconnected emotionally, the ability to engage in real and effective communication is diminished, thereby restricting the amount of trust and trustworthiness we are able to achieve.

Many people adopt a controlling approach *because* of their past experiences with letting go of control. If they believe that, at one point in their lives, they were taken advantage of, they don't want that to happen again. Going to the extreme, they make sure that they have the reins and clutch them tightly, not just around sharp turns, but also during the calm and smooth paths on their journeys. Though they may not recognize it, they are treating others just the way they believe they were treated in the past. It is like the abused child syndrome, where it is often abused children who become abusers themselves later in life. Likewise, overly controlling people often were, themselves, overly controlled by others.

Consider the case of Harry, a new editor of a regional business publication. When he was a young man he learned the journalism ropes from his father, a prominent managing editor of a local newspaper. His father had very high editorial and ethical standards and was exacting with his staff (including Harry). Harry witnessed lots of micromanaging by his father, from having to approve every word written, every advertisement sold, and every source's credibility. When Harry joined his new firm as a manager himself, he drew on his father's approach as his model for managing his new staff. As you might imagine, it did not go over very well. Harry's over-controlling style angered his employees and even his own boss to the point that he lost several award-winning journalists to competitors because of it.

Being a Control Freak often ensures that you prevail, at least for the moment, even if it means using manipulation, lies, and dishonesty. Unfortunately, it may also mean that you would do anything to get your way. But such behavior usually results in losing the power given to you by others, once your disingenuous behavior is recognized for what it really is—manipulation. But what is manipulation at its core?

## Manipulation is Still Just Control

> *Manipulation is a way to covertly influence someone with indirect, deceptive, or abusive tactics. Manipulation may seem benign or even friendly or flattering, as if the person has your highest concern in mind, but in reality it's to achieve an ulterior motive. Other times, it's veiled hostility, and when abusive methods are used, the objective is merely power.[8]*

[8] PsychCentral website, retrieved November 11, 2015 from http://psychcentral.com/lib/how-to-spot-manipulation/.

Manipulation is a form of control, but it is an indirect form, and that is what makes people who engage in it particularly irritating and difficult to deal with. George K. Simon, in his book, *In Sheep's Clothing*, distinguishes between people who overtly try to persuade by aggressively fighting or bullying others and those who, in his words, "…are subtle, underhanded or deceptive enough to hide [their] true intentions…avoiding any overt display of aggression while simultaneously intimidating others … is most often the vehicle for interpersonal manipulation."[9] At its core, manipulation is just *covert* control over others.

Those who manipulate can only do so if we allow them to know our most intimate fears. Manipulators generally use tactics that make just enough sense to have us doubt our hunch that we are being taken advantage of or abused. In addition, the tactics they employ keep us consciously on the defensive, and they are highly effective

---

[9] Simon, George K. *In Sheep's Clothing: Understanding and Dealing with Manipulative People*. Parkhurst Brothers Publishers, Inc., April 2010.

psychological weapons to which anyone can be vulnerable. They include guilt, blame, bribery, emotional blackmail, sympathy, and flattery. Unfortunately, our emotions often preclude us from recognizing a manipulator's hidden agenda or motives.

It is hard to think clearly when someone has you emotionally on the run. We all have weaknesses and insecurities that a clever manipulator might exploit. Sometimes we're aware of these weaknesses and how someone might use them to take advantage of us. Sometimes we're completely unaware of our biggest vulnerabilities. Manipulators often know us better than we know ourselves. They know which buttons to push, and when and how hard to push them. Bullying, both at school and at work, is one such example. Usually bullies focus on our most vulnerable selves to exploit our weaknesses, especially in front of others. Our lack of self-knowledge sets us up to be exploited and to act like victims. Over time, we become victims of our own beliefs. Like the character Jordan Belfort explained in the movie, *The Wolf of Wall Street*, "the only thing standing between you and your goal is the bullshit story you keep telling yourself as to why you can't achieve it."

We all have seen or heard about organizational and political leaders who have tried throughout their careers to ascend to the top of their organizations, but who have slipped down the ladder because of <u>how</u> they achieved that goal. Those who desire control because they do not want anyone else to have it, or because they believe that only through controlling others can they achieve their own goals, have a distorted sense of what true leadership is.

## Symptoms of a Control Freak

At their core, overly controlling people do not know *who they really are*, because they have a distorted view of reality and do not see their own fallibility. People with a high need for control often (1) believe they have the answers to, and the responsibility for, everyone's problems (e.g., the "I, alone, can fix it" mentality), (2) become overly anxious working for others or delegating work to others (e.g., "No one can do this as well as me"), (3) become socially isolated, often being seen as egotistical and narcissistic, (4) are often oblivious to nonverbal cues from others, because they dwell at the center of their own universe, (5) become overwhelmed by problems, partially because they have perfectionist tendencies and procrastinate dealing with problems unless they have the perfect "fix," and partially because they deny the reality of what is really going on until it is too late to do much about it, (6) are overly defensive to the criticisms of others (i.e., they take everything personally) or they blame others when things do not go as planned, and (7) convince themselves that they are correct in taking control *because* of the response of others to their behavior (e.g., lack of openness in communication, emotional or physical withdrawal, and lack of support). Take the *Are You a Control Freak or Approval-holic* assessment in Chapter 4 to see if <u>you</u> are high in control needs!

How you deal with Control Freaks is determined by first understanding the tendencies listed previously. Let's look at three of the more prominent ones: being a know-it-all, micromanaging others, and refusing to be held accountable or blaming others.

*I Have the Answer to Your Problem*

One of the most annoying tendencies of over-controlling people is that they believe they have the answer for everything. They are the "Mr. Fix-its" of our organizations and our lives. Moreover, they believe that they have the obligation and responsibility to solve everyone's problems. Where does this come from?

First, Control Freaks do not always recognize their own fallibility, nor do they always see how situational contexts influence problems and solutions. For example, if they once have solved a problem a certain way, they believe that is the way to solve it…always. Even if the problem they encounter looks similar to one they've had or seen before, the situation is likely to be different.

Because Control Freaks have a distorted view of reality (i.e., they see the world as a place that threatens their control), they attempt to maintain control by relying on the past successes they have had, even when the environment or the problem itself may have changed. As Albert Einstein so famously said, *"We can't solve problems by using the same kind of thinking we used when we created them."* One example of this is the focus on maintaining or bringing back jobs in the fossil fuel industry, despite the fact that science and economists suggest that more jobs will be created by expanding to cleaner energy approaches.

Ian Mitroff and Abraham Silvers, in their 2009 book, *Dirty Rotten Strategies*, extend the idea to which problems Control Freaks even focus on: "The trouble is that the problems one already knows how to solve may bear little resemblance to the problems one actually needs to solve." [10]

Harvard decision theorist Howard Raiffa labeled this the

error of "solving the wrong problem precisely." Many

managers, for example, focus on money to address employee

turnover, despite the fact that the problems causing turnover

are usually related less to wages and more to equitable

treatment, respect, and cultural fit. [11]

Second, Control Freaks have taken on solving

problems so that they make sure they can implement

whatever solution is adopted. In other words, if I come up

with a solution, I probably understand it and what is required

to put it into effect; therefore, I feel more in control. If,

instead, you decide on the solution, I may not be able to

actually do it, and that uncertainty threatens my control over

the situation.

Third, Control Freaks like being seen as a "Mr. Fix-

it." It is validation for their egos (or, in some cases, denial of

[10] Mitroff, I.I. and Silvers, A. (2009). *Dirty Rotten Strategies.* Stanford University Press: Stanford Business Books, Preface xv.
[11] Griffeth, P.H., and Griffeth, R. (1992). *Employee Turnover*. Cincinnati: South-Western Publishing.

their fears). But seen in a more positive light, it can also be a way for them to connect to people through doing something they believe is helpful to others.

Gary Chapman and Paul White's book, *The Five Languages of Appreciation in the Workplace*,[12] talks about expressing appreciation for employees who value Acts of Service. Pitching in to help out, rather than merely saying "thank you" or giving them a gift card, speaks volumes to some employees. It may be that Control Freaks, in general, have a tendency to value highly Acts of Service themselves and, therefore, providing solutions to others' problems is really speaking their own "love language."

The problem with trying to solve others' problems is that the solutions are not always the right solutions for that person. But a bigger problem a Control Freak is that this behavior takes away a chance for others to develop into good problem-solvers themselves. And, importantly, trying to "rescue" people from tough situations creates more victims—

---

[12] Chapman, G. and White, P. (2012). *The Five Languages of Appreciation in the Workplace*. Chicago, IL: Northfield Publishing.

dependent children or dependent employees—which, in turn, leads to the next challenge for a Control Freak: refusal to delegate and, ultimately, isolation.

*I'll Do It Myself, By Myself*

It is likely that most of you reading this book have been required at some point to work on a project with a Control Freak. The scenario usually starts with an immediate suggestion by the Control Freak that s/he is willing to take on the leadership/coordinator role. Usually everyone is fine with this in the beginning, since many of us don't want to be held responsible or accountable for everyone else's work, or we think that we don't have the time or resources to take on the job. So far, so good.

Next come the task assignments, meeting scheduling, and the actual project work itself. It is at this point that the Control Freak…well…freaks. Some people stop showing up at meetings; one or two members haven't turned in their work when expected; and there is always somebody who turns in garbage that has to be redone at the last minute.

What's a Control Freak to do?

One of the first tendencies is for the Control Freak to micromanage every member so closely that, one by one, each ultimately gives up and relinquishes control to the Control Freak. This abandonment of responsibility results in the very thing that is the Control Freak's justification for taking control in the first place: "No one but me can do this project right" or "Nobody is as committed to this as I am."

Following the unsuccessful attempt to get everyone on board, the Control Freak isolates himself, refusing to work with other members who, after trying to find out where the project stands, give up and let the Control Freak have at it. The project result is generally not as successful, the members resent their leader and each other, and the relationships among all the members deteriorates to the point that no one wants to work in a group ever again—especially the Control Freak. Then, if or when the product or process is questioned or criticized, the Control Freak is blind to the part he or she played in the debacle. This denial of responsibility results in another prominent challenge: denial of accountability.

*It's Not MY Fault!*

As mentioned previously, Control Freaks tend to be oblivious to nonverbal cues from others and have narcissistic tendencies, primarily because they dwell at the center of their own universe. As a result, they become socially isolated. At their core, narcissists have an inflated sense of their own importance and a lack of empathy for others. But behind this mask of confidence lies a fragile self-esteem that's vulnerable to the slightest criticism.

Because Control Freaks take all criticism personally, they have the tendency to shift responsibility and accountability to other people or to the context. It is the classic fundamental attribution error: they rationalize their failures as due to external causes (e.g., people, situations, lack of resources), but they attribute others' failures to internal causes (e.g., lack of ability, motivation, or inappropriate behaviors).[13] As a result, they do not accept the part they may have played in the unsuccessful endeavor.

Let's say your Chuck has a very high rate of turnover in her department. She may blame the amount of compensation she's able to offer, the poor quality of applicants, or the lack of training available. What she probably doesn't attribute high turnover to is her own controlling management style. And yet, we know that most turnover tends to be higher in environments where employees feel they are taken advantage of, where they feel undervalued or ignored, and where they feel helpless or unimportant. As is commonly stated, "people don't leave jobs, they leave managers."[14]

---

[13] Ross, L. (1977). The intuitive psychologist and his shortcomings: Distortions in the attribution process. In L. Berkowitz (Ed.), *Advances in experimental social psychology, Volume 10.* New York: Academic Presss.

[14] Higgenbottom, K. (2015). Bad bosses at the heart of employee turnover. Retrieved from http://www.forbes.com/sites/karenhigginbottom/2015/09/08/bad-bosses-at-the-heart-of-employee-turnover/#6861589e4075, February 17, 2017.

As a long-researched personality trait, Locus of Control[15] also helps explain why Control Freaks blame others. The concept begins with an understanding that people tend to attribute outcomes either to their own abilities or to chance circumstances. People who have an *internal* locus of control believe that the outcomes of their actions are results of their own abilities. They also believe that actions have consequences, which makes them accept the fact that things happen, and it is ultimately up to them whether they exercise control over it or not.

People with an *external* locus of control tend to believe that the things which happen in their lives are not under their control. They perceive that most of their own behaviors are a result of external factors, such as fate, luck, the influence of powerful others, or a belief that the world is too complex for one to successfully control its outcomes.

---

[15] Rotter, J. B. (1966). Generalized expectancies for internal versus external control of reinforcement. *Psychological Monographs: General & Applied*, 80(1), 1-28.

Such people tend to blame others, rather than themselves, for undesirable outcomes.

Control Freaks, by strict locus of control and attribution interpretations, would seem to have an internal locus of control—but only when they are successful. However, the irony of this tendency is that a Control Freak's greatest fear is loss of control, and interpreting criticism as a personal attack leads him or her to readily attribute control to someone or something else external. In this way, they are able to both protect their perception of infallibility and justify their reasons for needing to take control: "If I had been doing this myself, none of this would have happened this way." Of course, when they do take control and are successful, their internal attribution of success is subsequently reinforced.

## Working on Your Need for Control

By now it is apparent that the primary underlying fear for Control Freaks is loss of control and that their primary response to that fear is trying to maintain control at all costs.

If you are a Control Freak yourself, here is an exercise to help you focus on the underlying beliefs and motivations for your need to control:

1. For the next 2-3 weeks, describe in written form (e.g., a journal) some examples of the control problems, fears, and situations you experience in your work, school, and family relationships.
2. For each of the problems identified in Step 1, list the beliefs (causes) that account for your need for control.
3. Identify behavior, beliefs, attitudes, and feelings that need to be changed in order to resolve the problem.

Here's a more specific example:

1. "At work today I was asked to completely change a report I worked on because my boss decided that she needed the information in a different format. Because I didn't want to change the report, I argued with her that the way I presented it made more sense."
2. My belief is that if I know the "right" way to do something, I am not willing to do it in a different way just because someone in authority tells me to.
3. I need to realize that I have to listen and consider someone else's opinion more openly. I must work on asking "why?" a requested change has me so defensive and on identifying what I need to do to reduce my feelings of defensiveness.


If Your Chuck is a Control Freak

If your Chuck is a Control Freak, there are some helpful things to minimize the negative consequences:

1. Always remain calm and avoid aggressive language. Monitor the anxiety levels of the controlling person, because it is usually under high levels of stress and anxiety when they most lose their coping skills. Offering to take something off their plate often helps calm them down.

2. Try respectfully approaching the person and explain that you understand and appreciate his/her concerns for the project and getting good outcomes and that you want them, too. Then go on to explain how their controlling behavior affects you in terms of your own motivation.

3. When the controlling person does relinquish control, praise him or her! Noticing the positive and acknowledging it may encourage them to want to do it again.

4. Recognize that sometimes the controlling person may not give you credit for your ideas or actions. This can be frustrating. However, sometimes for the "good of the order" it is better to have the solution than not to have it. Don't take it personally.

5. Finally, consider your own role in the person's controlling behavior. Have you done something (or failed to do something) that may have provoked such controlling behavior? Like the Control Freak, all of us are prone to make fundamental attribution errors.

Here are some specific things you might say:

- "I see you are very worried about being able to complete X. I'm happy to do Task A for you so you can focus on Task B."
- "When you ask me to give you my work so that you can rework everything I feel like you don't trust me to use my experience and qualifications for the good of the project, and that makes me feel less motivated to do my best work."
- "Thanks for trusting me with that task."

Now that we have a good idea about what makes a Control Freak tick, it's time to turn our attention to the other difficult person we must deal with—an Approval-holic.

# CHAPTER 3

## WHAT'S AN APPROVAL-HOLIC?

*A truly strong person does not need the approval of others any more than a lion needs the approval of sheep.*
                    –Vernon Howard, American Writer
                    and Spiritual Teacher (1918-1992)

The earliest relationships we have are with our parents and siblings. We learn to seek their approval for our behaviors, and to some extent for our feelings, at a very young age. Why is this?

One reason is that we want to be loved, and so we may see disapproval of our *behaviors* as really showing disapproval of *ourselves*. Child development experts recommend separating these two (self from behavior) when providing feedback to children.[16] But for many people who grew up with parents or teachers who, intentionally or unintentionally, linked the two, others' disagreement or

---

[16] Rudolph, K.D., Caldwell, M.S., and Conley, C.S. (2005). Need for approval and children's well-being. *Child Development*, 76, 2, pp. 309-323.

disapproval of their behavior is often viewed as disapproval of them as persons, unworthy of respect, dignity, and trust.

Several authors have demonstrated that individuals characterized by a high need for approval are more likely to conform to others' expectations and cultural values, and they are more easily influenced by others than those low in need for approval.[17] In essence, people with a high need for approval are protecting a vulnerable self-esteem. As adults, and especially as leaders, we need to learn to assume some responsibility for developing our own self-esteem without depending constantly on others to validate it. And we need to recognize the potential for this phenomenon in our employees as well.

While the need for approval may be a natural evolution in our development, it can become problematic when we cannot get enough affirmation of our self-worth by solely relying on others to provide it. Sometimes the problem develops because we don't get enough positive

[17] Cravens, R.W. (1975). The need for approval and the private versus public disclosure of self. *Journal of Personality*, 43, 3, pp. 503-514.

feedback from our parents, teachers, and peers. Receiving positive feedback helps us develop better social competence by motivating us to act in ways that encourage positive feedback to continue and by aiding our detection and accurate interpretation of social cues.[18]

However, there is a downside to having a view of self that is too positive. That is, if it isn't a realistic and true appraisal, we will not be as open to instruction and growth. Recent research, for example, has suggested that an extremely positive self-appraisal can sometimes be associated with poorer recall of negative events,[19] and this may result in a greater likelihood of distorting reality. For example, Justin A. Frank, M.D. discusses in his book, *Bush on the Couch: Inside the Mind of the President*, that President George W. Bush's "forgetfulness" about mistakes

---

[18] Rudolph et al. (2005).
[19] Rudolph, K.D. and Pickett, C.L. (2004). Need for approval and processing of social information. Unpublished manuscript.

or actions in his past was likely due to his mother's overly positive (and, not necessarily, accurate) affirmation of him.[20]

Carol Dweck, in her book, *Mindset: The New Psychology of Success*,[21] describes two mindsets: fixed or growth. A fixed mindset is one in which talents and abilities are viewed as immutable. In other words, you are who you are, your intelligence and talents are fixed from an early age, and your fate is to go through life avoiding challenge and failure. A growth mindset, on the other hand, is one in which you see yourself as a work in progress. In essence, overly praising intelligence and ability doesn't foster a healthy self-esteem, nor does it lead to accomplishment, but can actually jeopardize one's success.

On the other hand, the feedback we get early in life from the people we admire is often "improvement" feedback ("You need to get your grades up") or feedback that compares us with someone else ("What is with this "D" in

---

[20] Frank, J.A. (2004). *Bush on the Couch: Inside the Mind of the President,* NY: HarperCollins Publishers, Inc.
[21] Dweck, C.S. (2006). *Mindset: The New Psychology of Success.* NY: Random House LLC.

math? Your sister never had trouble with math."). Negative or comparative feedback can be particularly distressing for those persons whose self-worth is threatened by disapproval, because they have a tendency to overreact to, or place a disproportionate emphasis on, such judgments.[22] For the most part, many of us tend to pay more attention to negative feedback than we do to positive feedback. Over time, whether the distortion in our reality is positive or negative, we will become accustomed to that distortion.

Consider the experiment in which college students were asked to wear special eyeglasses for one month that turned everything upside down.[23] At first, they stumbled around, tripped over things, and generally had great difficulty with perceptual judgment. Their brain knew how things were supposed to be and rejected what their eyes were telling them. But, after just a few days they adjusted, and their brains became accustomed to their upside-down world. After an entire month, the students reported that the glasses posed

---

[22] Rudolph, et al. (2005).
[23] Reported in McGraw, P.C. (2005) *Self Matters*, Hyperion Press.

no challenge for them at all. In fact, they were able to navigate just as easily as their right-side-up counterparts! Ultimately, they began to see this previously distorted view as perfectly normal.

The same phenomenon holds true with our acceptance of approval or disapproval from those who are important to us. Over time, approval causes us to build our positive self-view and feel worthy and valued. However, if we experience continuing disapproval, we begin to believe it and feel distress whenever we receive "constructive criticism" or when we realize that we are not meeting others' expectations. The distress is real, but the reaction is counterfeit. This distress often leads us to try too hard to please another, which becomes annoying or is perceived by others as "kissing up." It also provides us with a million excuses for past behavior, allowing us to play "the victim," never appearing responsible for our decisions. Neither of these responses is healthy.

Becoming overly reliant on others' feedback has taught us to become dependent on them, not just to gain their approval, but also as models for what it means to be a "good" child, adult, parent, employee, or leader. One problem with this paradigm is that these models are often unrealistic or idealistic and can never really be emulated. Another problem is that we need to accept our strengths and challenges for what they really are, even if they are not "approved of" by others. Our realization that others may be better or worse than us at some things needs to be tempered by a similar recognition that we may be better or worse than they are at other things. This self-inventory is a solid foundation for recognizing the fullness of our potential for personal and professional development. The roadblocks to discovering this inventory, however, lie in our anxieties about, and fear of, disapproval.

Interestingly, Marianne Williamson implies that our need for approval may actually be fear of who we really are:

*Our greatest fear is not that we are inadequate,*
*but that we are powerful beyond measure.*

*It is our light, not our darkness, that frightens us.*
*We ask ourselves, Who am I to be brilliant,*
*gorgeous, handsome, talented and fabulous?*

*Actually, who are you not to be?*
*You are a child of God.*

*Your playing small does not serve the world.*
*There is nothing enlightened about shrinking*
*so that other people won't feel insecure around you.*

*We were born to make manifest the glory of God*
*within us.*
*It is not just in some; it is in everyone.*

*And, as we let our own light shine, we consciously*
*give*
*other people permission to do the same.*
*As we are liberated from our fear,*
*our presence automatically liberates others.*[24]

No one likes to be shunned or ostracized.

Particularly, no one likes to experience disapproval from

someone we admire or love. And yet, none of us is immune

to disagreements or questioning about what we think, how

we behave, or whom we choose to support. So what is it that

[24] Williamson, M. (1992). *A Return To Love: Reflections on the Principles of A Course in Miracles*, Harper Collins. From Chapter 7, Section 3 (Pg. 190-191).

distinguishes Approval-holics from those of us with low or moderate needs for approval?

Remember that most approval needs begin early in our lives. As a result, we are conditioned to want to please those we love, partly for the emotional connection with them and partly for the realization that we are dependent on them for our very existence. From a child's viewpoint, this is perfectly normal. But from an adult's perspective, it is not.

## Symptoms of an Approval-holic

As a result of these anxieties and fears, we tend to have a limited understanding of *who we really are*, because we are always trying to be something we are not or to behave in ways that lead to approval from others. As such, people with a high need for approval often (1) have low self-esteem, (2) give up on endeavors because they are convinced that whatever they do isn't "good enough," (3) are emotionally dependent on others for affirmation, (4) avoid conflict because of the fear of others' disapproval of their views or to avoid hurting the feelings of others, (5) fret over the potential consequences of decisions to the point that they can never make a decision, and (6) fear rejection and abandonment so much that they subjugate their own needs, feelings, and wants to those of others. For these people, approval is not simply desirable; it is *imperative,* like oxygen.

When we encounter those who have an extraordinarily high need for approval we often feel uncomfortable with being so needed that we avoid, or even flee, relationships with them. We see that their unending requirement for positive strokes paralyzes their decision-making. We feel guilty, because we haven't given them enough reinforcement, or we feel overwhelmed by our perceived obligation to rescue them. And, occasionally, we feel sorry for them to the point of dismissing most of what they say and do as being based on their need for approval and not on what is *real.* Ultimately, however, we stop trying to "save" them, we lose respect for them, and we may end up having an emotional chasm in our relationships with them, much like Alice's employees described in the following

scenario.

---

**Is Alice an Approval-holic?**

*Alice had just been promoted to Advertising Manager at a small magazine publishing company. She had worked side-by-side with the sales reps in the Advertising Department for several years, and felt as if they were her friends. In fact, she decided not to move into the Advertising Manager's private office upon her promotion, but to stay out in the bull pen with her "friends."*

*Soon, two of her employees were in disagreement about whose territory was whose, whose responsibility it was to proof the ads they sold, etc. They appealed to Alice to settle these disagreements, but Alice avoided the disputes by never directly addressing the issue or holding either of them accountable. The problems mounted, and ultimately both employees stopped talking to each other and to Alice.*

---

Clearly, Alice's need for the approval of her

employee "friends" drove her inability or unwillingness to

make managerial decisions in the Advertising Department.

She avoided the conflict, tried to take a non-involved

position, and generally created an emotional barrier between

herself and her employees. The most ironic thing about

people who are high in their need for approval is that they

create the very thing that makes them most afraid—losing the approval of others. Take the *Are You a Control Freak or Approval-holic* assessment in Chapter 4 to see if you are high in approval needs.

Let's look at some of these Approval-holic symptoms in more depth so that we can begin to figure out how to engage with them in productive ways. There are many, but for now we'll focus on just three: low self-esteem, decidophobia, and fear of conflict.

### *I'm Not Good Enough*

At the core of an Approval-holic's fears is low self-esteem. Self-esteem is based on the experiences you have had in life, and the messages sent by these experiences about who you are. Positive experiences tend to create positive self-beliefs. However, if our experiences have been negative, our beliefs about ourselves are likely to be negative, too.

Crucial experiences that help to form our beliefs about ourselves often occur early in life and are interpreted through the eyes of a child and, therefore, are often biased and inaccurate. Some of them were positive (e.g., receiving praise for good grades or exemplary behavior), but some of them were very negative (e.g., failing to meet parental or peer standards, being discriminated against because of your family or ethnic/racial group, experiencing an absence of praise or affection). Of course, negative beliefs about oneself can be caused by experiences later in life, too, such as workplace bullying or intimidation, abusive relationships, or traumatic events.

The problem with these previous and persistent negative experiences is that it causes Approval-holics to give undue weight to things that are consistent with these beliefs and to discount anything that is not. Basically this means that the focus is on what is <u>wrong</u> about them, ignoring what is right about them. Approval-holics also have a tendency to distort meaning in what they do experience, even if that experience is positive. For example, getting a compliment about her appearance might cause an Approval-holic to think that the person thought she was unattractive before or that the person was being disingenuous.

The result of low self-esteem is that an employee or manager does not believe s/he "deserves" any responsibility, rewards, or recognition. Unlike the Control Freak who has the tendency to think of herself as "Master of the Universe," an Approval-holic thinks of himself as "Slave of the Universe." In other words, s/he is undeserving, incapable, and not good enough to take on the task, hold the position, keep the relationship, or tackle the responsibility they've been given. That is why they are constantly seeking the approval from others to overcome their own perceptions of who they are and what they are capable of doing.

If your Chuck is like many other Chucks, he seems overly concerned with validation from his boss, his peers, or his direct reports. For example, perhaps he always tries to flatter his boss, telling her how well she handled a situation; or maybe he spends too much time preparing a report or figures for a meeting so that he can be seen as a "hard worker" or "an overachiever." Whatever his approach, the underlying motivation is to get acclimation from someone else to validate his perception that he is "not good enough."

*Whatever You Want is Fine with Me*

Making a decision requires confidence and a degree of certainty. And some decisions require a great deal of courage. When tough decisions with serious consequences are called for, it can be difficult for some people to act. The fear of making the wrong decision can cause a sort of mental paralysis; at its worst, it can ultimately create a phobia called "decidophobia"—the fear of making *any* decision.

For Approval-holics, this is a common occurrence. The notion, "whatever you want is fine with me," really masks the underlying fear of making the wrong decision and, ultimately, losing the approval of others. Remember that it isn't that Approval-holics don't care about the outcomes and consequences of the decision itself—they do. But the fear of disapproval overshadows the practical (and perhaps positive) results that the decision might have.

Perhaps many of you reading this have sat in meetings in which a decision is supposed to be made. The chair or facilitator for the meeting asks for input, maybe even for someone to act as a devil's advocate. If an Approval-holic is in that meeting, it is likely that he or she will agree with whomever has the most power.

Take the classic "Approval-holic" situation faced by John F. Kennedy during the Bay of Pigs Invasion in 1962. The idea was to send in Cuban exiles to topple Fidel Castro. Kennedy asked his top advisers whether he should authorize such an invasion, and all concurred. However, each person in that meeting was unwilling to challenge it as a bad idea. One advisor even presented serious objections to the invasion in a memorandum to the president, but he suppressed his doubts at the meetings. The invasion was a disaster, primarily because no one was willing to go against what he thought was President Kennedy's desire to invade.

By going along with what others want or refusing to decide at all, the Approval-holic unrealistically believes s/he will avoid any unpleasantness, criticism, or conflict. Unfortunately, it is often the opposite result, creating more conflict and tension that if s/he had voiced a dissenting opinion. It is these interpersonal outcomes that are feared most and lead to the central plea of the Approval-holic: "Can't we all just get along?"

*Can't We All Just Get Along?*

In essence, we all have a similar response to conflict: we don't like it. But, for an Approval-holic, an interpersonal conflict can be serious enough to cause anxiety and insecurity. When anxiety or insecurity is first experienced, as sentient human beings we have a choice between reactivity (i.e., flight or fright) and reflection. If we do not make a choice, our brain's default mode is to be reactive. From this anxiety and insecurity, we experience inadequacy (we don't know what to do) and a drop in self-esteem (we don't feel good about ourselves). And for an Approval-holic, these experiences trigger the ultimate fear: loss of others' approval.

As a result, the Approval-holic often chooses to avoid conflict all together or to accommodate the person with whom he or she is having the conflict. Neither one of these is a healthy response, according to Kenneth W. Thomas and Ralph H. Kilmann, authors of the Thomas-Kilmann Conflict Mode Instrument (TKI).[25]

For starters, avoiding conflict is both unassertive and uncooperative. That is, the person avoids both his own concerns as well as those of the other individual. In the heat of the moment, avoiding conflict is sometimes an appropriate strategy; it might mean diplomatically sidestepping an issue, postponing dealing with an issue until a later time, or simply withdrawing from a conflict situation all together. But Approval-holics who routinely avoid conflict lose or never gain the respect of colleagues or

---

[25] Thomas, K. W., & Kilmann, R. H. (1974). Thomas-Kilmann Conflict Mode Instrument. Mountain View, CA: Xicom, a subsidiary of CPP, Inc.

managers and, as a result, their perceived inability to confront interpersonal conflict eventually erodes their trustworthiness.

In accommodation, the person neglects his own concerns (unassertive) in order to satisfy the concerns of the other person (cooperative). Basically, there is an element of self-sacrifice in this approach. Accommodating might take the form of selflessness, obeying another person's order when one would prefer not to, or yielding to another's point of view even when one doesn't agree. Although an accommodation mode may garner some initial approval through its perceived cooperation with others, over time it is seen as indecisive and wimpy behavior, resulting in loss of confidence in the Approval-holic's ability to stand up for himself.

## Working on Your Need for Approval

By now it is apparent that the primary underlying fear for Approval-holics is loss of approval from others and that their primary response to that fear is continuously seeking approval or avoiding disapproval at all costs. If you are an

Approval-holic yourself, here is an exercise to help you focus

on the underlying beliefs and motivations for social approval:

1. For the next 2-3 weeks, describe in written form (e.g., a journal) some examples of the approval problems and situations you experience in your work, school, and family relationships.
2. For each of the problems identified in Step 1, list the beliefs (causes) that account for your need for approval.
3. Identify behavior, beliefs, attitudes, and feelings that need to be changed in order to resolve the problem.

Here's a more specific example:

- "At work today I was asked to completely change a report I worked on because my boss decided that she needed the information in a different format. I am sure she doesn't think how I did it is good enough."
- "The last time I turned in work she asked me to redo it because it had some errors. I'm sure she just said she needed a different format because I didn't do it right again."
- "I need to take my boss' words at face value. I must realize that "I am not the report" and that a critique of my work is not a critique of me, personally."

**You might also try this:**

1. Identify a person in your work life sphere and a person in your personal life sphere who you really want to think you are great.
2. For each person, list the characteristics they have that you most admire.

3. Now, for each characteristic you list, rate yourself on that characteristic (1=Low, 5=High). If you cannot be objective, ask a person close to you to rate you.
4. Develop a list of positive affirmation self-talk scripts you can use to affirm yourself on the highly-rated characteristics. Do not think further about the characteristics rated "low." Your task in this exercise is to work on understanding the relationship between what you value in others and your own perceptions of those characteristics in you.

## If Your Chuck is an Approval-holic

If your Chuck is an Approval-holic, there are some

helpful things to minimize the negative consequences:

1. Always remain calm and avoid aggressive language. Monitor the anxiety levels of the controlling person, because it is usually under high levels of stress and anxiety when they most struggle with questioning themselves or their decisions.
2. Try respectfully approaching the person and explain that you understand and appreciate his/her concerns for the project and getting good outcomes and that you want them, too. Then, remind them that you have every confidence that they can do the work. Offer your help or resources if they would like them.
3. When the work is turned in correctly, on time, etc., thank them for their good work. Do not overly praise, but recognize the work itself (not the person). Noticing the positive and acknowledging it may encourage them to want to do it again.
4. Finally, consider your own role in the person's dependent or "victim" behavior. Have you done something (or failed to do something) that may have led them to fear your disapproval? Remember that all

of us are prone to make fundamental attribution errors.

Now it is time to see where YOU stand in your needs for Control and Approval. In the next chapter you will be able to assess yourself (you might also wish to give the assessment to someone you are close to or must work closely with) and find out what challenges you might face in working with others, leading a team, or even getting along with your child or significant other!

# CHAPTER 4

## DISCOVERING YOUR DOMINANT NEED

The truth is that we all need to feel some approval from others and to feel some control over ourselves and our surroundings. What is important for our discussion here is to understand how those needs are balanced and to what extent they dictate our behaviors. Obviously, everyone's underlying needs play out in different ways, but our predominant need will tend to emerge most often in our workplace behaviors, particularly when we are under pressure or stress, when we find ourselves threatened by someone or something, or when the situation does not clearly indicate the action we should take.

This is what is known in psychology as the Cognitive-Affective Processing System (CAPS) that was proposed by Walter Mischel and Yuichi Shoda in 1995.[26] In their view, an individual's behavior can be understood best

---

[26] Mischel, W. & Shoda, Y. (1995). A cognitive-affective system theory of personality: Reconceptualizing situations, dispositions, dynamics, and invariance in personality structure. *Psychological Review*, 102, 246-268.

by looking at the interaction between personality and the context or situation. Relevant to our discussion here, that means that whichever need is more dominant for a person—approval or control—it will be more obvious in some situations than in others. The key is recognizing the triggers in situations so that one's control or approval tendencies can be better managed.

For example, if your Chuck has a dominant need for approval, it probably is particularly apparent any time he has to make a decision that has potentially negative consequences for someone whose approval he seeks. A Chuck with a dominant need for control can be identified right away when she is challenged in her decision or when she has to delegate important work to a direct report. Interestingly, there are even more specific ways people with high needs for approval and control can be identified.

## Does Your Chuck Seek Approval or Avoid Disapproval?

One interesting aspect of Need for Approval is the
fact that studies have indicated that there are really two
dimensions within the primary need for approval construct: a
desire to avoid negative evaluation (i.e., Avoid Disapproval)
and a desire to obtain positive evaluation (i.e., Seek
Approval).[27,28] Generally, people with low self-esteem tend
to avoid disapproval, while seeking approval is more typical
of those with higher self-esteem. There are some negative
outcomes associated with both. For example, if Chuck acts
to avoid social disapproval, he is more likely to become
stressed or even depressed, particularly if the feared
disapproval comes from someone very important to him.
However, if he has more of a tendency to seek approval from
others, he probably demonstrates more ingratiating behavior
that may also include lying and deception to gain favor from

---

[27] Berger, S.E., Levin, P., Jacobson, L.I., and Millham, J. (1977). Gain
approval or "Avoid Disapproval": Comparison of motive strengths in
high need for approval scorers. *Journal of Personality,* 45(3), 458.
[28] Paulhus, D. L. (1984). Two-component models of socially desirable
responding. *Journal of Personality and Social Psychology*, 46, 598-609.

those he's trying to impress. Either or both of these approval

forms undermines his trustworthiness with others.

## Does Your Chuck Struggle More with Self-control or Control of Others and Situations?

Like Need for Approval, studies have also found that

there are multiple Need for Control dimensions (e.g., Control

of Self and Control of Others/Situations).[29]  Your Chuck may

be highly committed to being in charge of every situation and

to avoid situations where someone else is in control.  Other

Chucks may have an urge to control people's behavior and

their performance outcomes.  And some Chucks may

struggle with controlling their own emotions or responses.

The bottom line is that both positive behaviors (such as

having a high need to achieve and compete) and negative

behaviors (such as dominance and an unwillingness to defer

---

[29] Gebhardt, W.F. and Brosschot, J.F. (2002).  Desirability of control: psychometric properties and relationships with locus of control personality, coping, and mental and somatic complaints in three Dutch samples. *European Journal of Personality,* 16(6), 423-438.

to others) are typical of those with both types of a high need for control.

It might be interesting to understand your own tendencies, too, so that you can see which need is more dominant for you. Take the assessment at the end of this chapter—*Are You a Control Freak or an Approval-holic?* Then plot your scores on the matrix. The quadrant your "dot" is in indicates your dominant tendency toward need for approval and need for control.

## The Relationship between Approval and Control

One important thing to know is that need for approval and need for control are not opposite ends of the same spectrum. That is to say, it isn't true that people high in approval are necessarily low in control or vice versa. Instead, think of them as two completely different needs that can vary independently of each other. To better illustrate the relationship, consider the model below. I have given each quadrant a distinctive name to highlight the differences:

Dictator, Manipulator, Spectator, and Facilitator.


*Need for Approval*

|  | Low | High |
|---|---|---|
| **High**<br>***Need for***<br>***Control*** | **Dictator** | **Manipulator** |
| **Low** | **Facilitator** | **Spectator** |


## Dictator

"Dictators" have a high need for control coupled with

a low need for approval.  This indicates that they really aren't

that concerned with what people think about them or how

they accomplish things.  Rather, they are more concerned

with keeping everything orderly, precise, and predictable for

their own sanity.  In essence, they may be afraid that if they

don't take care of things, they will never get done.  As a

result, although they may be better able to accomplish an outcome, they may not be viewed as trustworthy regarding the process. That is, people are not as likely to feel involved in, or knowledgeable about, what is occurring and, therefore, may withdraw emotionally or physically from the task or project. As a result, Dictators are likely to become even more controlling, thereby reinforcing their belief that "If I don't do it, then no one will." This may, in turn, causes others to withdraw even more, resulting in even less communication and continuing the downward spiral of distrust for their motives or approaches.

As an example, think about the most controlling person you know—family member or professional colleague. Does he or she tell you what's going on with a project or event, or do you have to find out from someone else or, worse, when it is a done deal? Do you feel comfortable working on a project with the person, or do you tend to let them have their own way and just do whatever they want to do? And, if you have a more personal relationship with someone who is controlling, do you feel free to express your feelings or do you hold back, afraid of what might happen if you are honest?

At their worst, Dictators push us away, lose our trust, and in some extreme cases actually frighten us. But, at their best, they can usually accomplish some fairly complex outcomes on time and within budget. And in a crisis, you wouldn't want anyone else! The problem is that most of the time we are not in a crisis and prefer a more inclusive approach to work, projects, and decisions.

## Manipulator

"Manipulators" have high needs for both control and approval. They reason that if they can control people and situations, things will turn out as they want them to be. On the other hand, because they also need others' approval, they may play on your sympathy and concern by appearing to be a martyr or an overworked and unappreciated victim.

Manipulators present reality the way they want others to see it, rather than the way it really is, in order to avoid conflict.

Sometimes, if a Manipulator senses another person is pulling away from them, they may even feign a problem or need that they believe will get the other person involved with again. Such behavior is manipulative and unauthentic. The result is that the genuineness of their motives (i.e., why they are doing what they are doing) begins to be questioned. Once this happens, questions about trustworthiness begin to surface as well.

Some of you may think this title of "Manipulator" is a bit harsh. Who wants to be known as a Manipulator? But the bottom line is that individuals who are high in both need for control and need for approval are at war within themselves to maintain control AND to make sure that they have others' approval. Thus, they are always trying to balance the two. That is why it often requires some manipulation of the people or the situation involved in order to maintain that balance of power and influence.

As an example, Machiavelli wrote of Emperor Maximillian I, the Roman Emperor of the 1500's in his book, *The Prince*, that he was secretive and never consulted others. But once he ordered his plans and met with dissent from his subjects, he immediately changed the plans. This is what Manipulators do—follow whichever way the wind blows.

## Spectator

"Spectators" have a low need for control, but a high need for approval; therefore, they are likely to let others control and direct them. Maybe they do this so that they feel a sense of importance, feel valued and, ultimately, are regarded positively. Or, since their need for approval, fear of rejection, and feelings of insecurity are so high, they may become immobilized without the direction, support, and nurturing of the person upon whose approval they have become dependent. Indecision and paralysis set in because of a fear not being "right" or not fitting in. They become, in essence, a spectator of their own lives. As a result, Spectators often lose a sense of personal identity, uniqueness, or independence, so the very approval they are seeking is often withheld, primarily because others do not see them as competent enough to function without direction or approval from others, causing the very thing they most fear: disapproval.

## Facilitator

"Facilitators" have low needs for both control and approval, and they probably have the healthiest balance between the two. First, they are better able to keep in check many self-destructive, addictive, obsessive, irrational, and unacceptable behaviors. Second, because Facilitators don't have a tendency to be manipulative, helpless, intimidating, domineering, or overly dependent on others, they are able to keep their relationships with followers, peers, and bosses in a healthy balance of give and take. They draw appropriate boundaries between themselves and their co-workers, boss, and followers. Facilitators encourage and empower others to be independent and to use their inner reserves of competence, skills, and abilities to solve their own problems. In essence, they are able to allow others to develop their own potential without their own being threatened. Most importantly, they are able to demonstrate their inner desire to be a mature, responsible adult with a sense of personal mastery, autonomy, and competency over their own life. As a result, Facilitators tend to engender the highest level of trust from others.

Whatever your more dominant need, recognize that it did not develop overnight. You may struggle with approval or control your entire life, but it is a fundamental struggle that will help you develop into someone who is able to inspire and support others toward their greatest achievements.

## What's Next?

The next several chapters explore how control and approval needs influence the prominent challenges mentioned in the first part of the book. First, we'll discuss the "myth of perfection" that underlies many of these

challenges. Then, we'll look at the ramifications of these

challenges on trustworthiness within work relationships and

suggest some ways to address them, including what to do

about them if they arise with your "Chuck."

# Are You a Control Freak or an Approval-holic?

**Think about your workplace as you formulate your answers below.**
Read each statement and circle "T" if the statement is <u>generally</u> true for
you and "F" if the statement is <u>generally</u> false for you as you deal with
people at work. There are no right or wrong answers. Be as honest as
you can.

| | | |
|---|---|---|
| T<br>F | 1. | If someone disapproves of me, I feel like I'm not very worthwhile. |
| T<br>F | 2. | It's extremely important to be liked by nearly everyone. |
| T<br>F | 3. | I avoid making mistakes in front of others at all costs. |
| T<br>F | 4. | I believe I need the approval of others more than most people do. |
| T<br>F | 5. | I need others to approve of me in order to really feel good about myself. |
| T<br>F | 6. | It bothers me a lot to learn that someone doesn't like me. |
| T<br>F | 7. | If people I respect act disappointed in me, I dwell on it for days. |
| T<br>F | 8. | I seem to need everyone's approval before I can make an important decision. |
| T<br>F | 9. | I'm strongly motivated by the praise and approval I get from others. |
| T<br>F | 10. | I'm deeply concerned about what others think of me at work. |
| T<br>F | 11. | I get very defensive when criticism is directed at me. |
| T<br>F | 12. | I need to have everyone like me, even though I don't really like everyone. |
| T<br>F | 13. | It only takes one person's criticism or disapproval in a group to upset me, even when everyone else is giving me praise. |
| T<br>F | 14. | I have trouble asking others for favors and tend to apologize a lot. |
| T<br>F | 15. | If I can control others, they will do what I want them to do. |
| T<br>F | 16. | I hate to feel out of control or to lose control. |

| | |
|---|---|
| T<br>F | 17. I believe that if things don't go my way, I have to work harder. |
| T<br>F | 18. It bothers me to have people see my true feelings, so I struggle to control my feelings in front of others. |
| T<br>F | 19. I often step into a situation when I see something that needs to be fixed. |
| T<br>F | 20. When I know in my own mind how something should be done, I work at trying to get it to be that way. |
| T<br>F | 21. I am afraid that if I don't take care of something, it won't get done. |
| T<br>F | 22. I tend to convey an "It's my way or the highway" approach with people who refuse to do something that needs to be done. |
| T<br>F | 23. When I feel intimidated, I compensate by taking more control of the situation. |

*How to Score and Interpret Your Answers:* Fill in the boxes on the next page with the number of "T" answers and total at the bottom of each column. [Higher scores indicate which dimension is more problematic for you.] Then add both approval scores together and both control scores together to get "Total Approval" and "Total Control" scores. Plot these "Total" Scores on the next page.

# Scoring Your Approval and Control Needs

| Seek Approval | Avoid Disapproval | Control Self | Control Others |
|---|---|---|---|
| 1. | | | |
| 2. | | | |
| | 3. | | |
| 4. | | | |
| 5. | | | |
| 6. | | | |
| | 7. | | |
| 8. | | | |
| 9. | | | |
| 10. | | | |
| | 11. | | |
| 12. | | | |
| 13. | | | |
| | 14. | | |
| | | | 15. |
| | | 16. | |
| | | 17. | |
| | | | 18. |
| | | 19. | |
| | | | 20. |
| | | 21. | |
| | | | 22. |
| | | | 23. |
| | | | |
| TOTAL APPROVAL (add above 2 | | TOTAL CONTROL (add above | |

*If your Approval score is between 11-14, you have a high need for approval from others*
*If your Approval score is between 6-10, you have a moderate need for approval from others.*
*If your Approval score is 5 or below, you have a low need for approval from others.*
*If your Control score is between 7-9, you have a high need for control from others*
*If your Control score is between 4-6, you have a moderate need for control from others.*
*If your Control score is 3 or below, you have a low need for control from others.*

## Plot It Yourself!

Using your "Total Approval' and "Total Control" scores, plot to see where you fit in the typologies. For example, a "12" on Approval and a "7" on Control puts you in the "Manipulator" category.

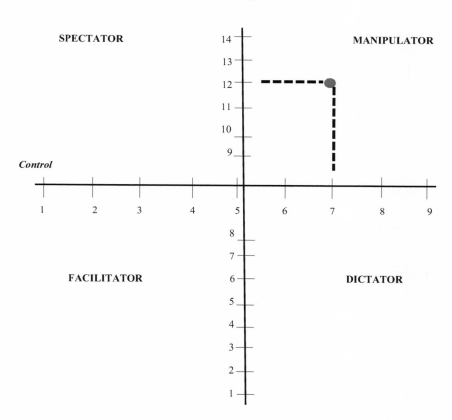

# CHAPTER 5

## WHY CHUCK DRIVES YOU CRAZY

*Life is like photography; you can't develop without the negative.* – Quincy Jones, composer

In Hans Christian Andersen's tale, *The Emperor's New Clothes*, it was particularly difficult for the townspeople to admit that the Emperor was naked. Why did everyone (including the Emperor himself) say they saw clothes that weren't there?

The answer lies in some very primary aspects of the human condition: anxiety and fear. We fear appearing stupid or unfit for a job; we fear receiving disapproval or scorn from others; we are anxious about reality when it poses unpleasant or seemingly insurmountable challenges. In other words, we are afraid of being seen as imperfect or lacking in some way. We want to be seen as the best (or, at least, highly competent) at our tasks, our jobs, and our relationships.

## The Myth of Perfection

Sadly, it is often organizations and our societal culture that promote the myth that we ought to be perfect if we wish to be successful, particularly if we aspire to a leadership role. Consider the media's microscopic evaluation of political candidates and officeholders, Supreme Court nominees, actors and actresses, clergy, and business leaders. While media scrutiny may provide more engaged readers or viewers, it is not healthy or encouraging to would-be leaders. Emphasizing flaws in character, practices, decisions, and behaviors leaves us with a perception that only "perfect" people should be leaders; anyone else is not good enough to lead our companies, our schools, our places of worship, our social service organizations, our economies, or our countries.

Clearly, everyone wants to avoid looking stupid and incompetent. But authentic people do not deny what is really going on in their relationships with the world or in their organizations. They recognize that they do not know everything, nor do they have a monopoly on the truth. The reality is that *there is no perfect leader or perfect employee*! All people have both burdens and blessings—strengths and challenges, as it were—that are a part of who they are. Moreover, it is important that we not only identify which strengths and challenges reside in us, but also figure out what got us to that point. We want to develop our strengths and gifts, but we also want to work on the challenges that are concerns for us in our professional roles and personal lives.

Consider a "Chuck" who has helped his organization get out of deepening debt, has championed zero-based budgeting, and has advocated for allocating administrative costs (e.g., electricity, office rent, cleaning, etc.) across revenue-generating departments. In other words, he is considered to have great strengths in finance. But his direct reports find him demeaning and rude, and several have requested transfers to a different location or have quit the organization all together. Obviously, finance "Chuck" has financial savvy as a strength, but he also is challenged by interpersonal and managerial relationships.

Marcus Buckingham and Donald Clifton in their best-selling book, *Now, Discover Your Strengths*, maintain that people shouldn't worry too much about their challenges or weaknesses. Instead, they should concentrate on developing their strengths. Buckingham and Clifton, themselves, view challenges and weaknesses as things that get in the way of excellent performance.[30] To the extent that a job requires behaviors, skills, or attitudes that one does not possess or is not very proficient at demonstrating, these authors suggest "managing around" those weaknesses and challenges.

While Buckingham and Clifton are correct that building on one's strengths is motivating and will improve overall performance, my contention is that unless one acknowledges the murky waters we fear plunging into, we

---

[30] Buckingham, M. and Clifton, D.O. (2001) *Now, Discover Your Strengths!* The Free Press.

can never fully develop our true potential. This is the challenge both for our Chucks at work and also for ourselves.

First, the problem with only "managing around" challenges is that many jobs and relationships require us to demonstrate a number of talents and skills that we do not currently possess. Therefore, it becomes virtually impossible to "manage around" something we don't have. If "financial" Chuck is required to engage frequently with his direct reports, but he is demeaning and rude to them, he is not going to be able to overcome that weakness by substituting it or "managing around" it with his excellent financial skills or strategies.

Second, as many of us know, trying to hide from others those things we are not very good at is difficult. If we view "managing around" as a means of masking these challenges, we probably won't be very successful, as most people can see behind those masks. In fact, it is tantamount to the Emperor's new clothes: everyone recognizes our challenges, even if they don't say that they do. And that is one sure-fire way to be seen as not authentic. As a result, others begin to wonder what else we may be hiding from them, which leads to an erosion of the trustworthiness and credibility we are seeking to achieve.

Remember our first "Chuck," the architect and project manager? His fear of disapproval might cause him to avoid difficult conversations about performance with his blue-collar subordinates, and this will likely affect his ability to be successful at getting his construction crew to solve problems, as well as his own motivation to continue in a supervisory role. And our second Chuck's need for control might cause the retail associates in her store to resent her bossiness and her self-centeredness, leading to emotional withdrawal for both Chuck and her subordinates. In both cases, the refusal to confront the "myth of perfection" is at the heart of their basic fear and anxiety: loss of approval or loss of control. And both of these fears play out in Chuck's behaviors which, of course, are the ones that drive you crazy!

## Plunging Below the Surface

The reality is that many of us live only marginally. This was Freud's definition of psychoneurosis: we limit how we live so that we can limit the amount of anxiety that we experience. We shut down the centers of creative thinking and, in effect, we halt progress and growth of the self. But no significant decision, whether personal or organizational, has ever been undertaken without a commitment to wade through anxiety and uncertainty.

One of the gravest problems in life is self-limitation. We create defense mechanisms to protect us from the anxiety that comes with the freedom to define ourselves. Anxiety reminds us of our huge responsibility to choose who we are and to define our place in the world. Therefore, because of such anxiety, we become unable to fulfill our potential, and that often creates even more fear, tension, and use of defense mechanisms. As Tolkien wrote, *A man that flies from his fear may find that he has only taken a shortcut to meet it.*[31]

Maslow, in his view of human potential, believed that the self-actualized person is not an ordinary person with something added, but an ordinary person with nothing taken away. He wrote that the average person is a full human being with dampened and inhibited powers and capacities:

> *All individuals have an inborn urge to become a complete person; that is, they have the tendency toward developing their uniqueness and singularity, discovering their personal identities, and striving for the full actualization of their potentials. To the extent that they fulfill their potentials as persons, they experience the deepest joy that is possible in human experience, for nature has intended them to do so.* [32]

Of course, the hardest part for Control Freaks and Approval-holics is that their fears and anxieties are almost always irrational. That is, it is usually impossible to reason

---

[31] Tolkien, J.R.R. (published posthumously in 2007). *The Children of Húrin.* New York: Houghton Mifflin Harcourt.

[32] Cole, M.B. (1993). The existential-humanistic approach, In *Group dynamics in occupational therapy: the theoretical basis and practice application of group treatment.* Thorofare, NJ: Slack Inc., p. 49.

fear out of existence; otherwise, the fear probably would have already been dealt with long ago!  David Whyte, in his wonderful book, *The Heart Aroused*, uses the Old English epic, *Beowolf*, to examine modern fears and anxieties of corporate life.

Beowolf is an allegory of the journey into one's deeper psyche and the monsters that one finds there.  In this poem, the prince and warrior, Beowulf, travels around the world offering his services to defeat the enemies of foreign kings.  He is retained by the King of Denmark to rid the kingdom of Grendel, a diabolical swamp creature, which he bravely does.  Interestingly, Whyte argues that Beowolf's larger challenge lies in defeating Grendel's mother, who pursues Beowolf after he has killed her son, Grendel.  In Whyte's words,

> *It is not the thing you fear that you must deal with, it is the mother of the thing you fear.  The very thing that has given birth to the nightmare…You can blame your mother, you can blame your father and his father for the problems with which you are destined*

*to wrestle, but ultimately you are the one in whom*
*they have made a home. You are the one who must*
*say, "Thus far and no farther," and then go down*
*and confront them yourself.* [33]

Like Beowolf, Control Freaks and Approval-holics
must recognize and deal with, first and foremost, the causes
of their fears and anxieties about performing effectively,
before they can even try to do things that "self-help" books
suggest: set goals, listen more intently to others, delegate
more, build consensus, resolve conflicts, and so on.
Moreover, this must also precede the work in developing
strengths and inner resources, for such understanding will
help with their development, too.

Ultimately, no one can develop authentically without
understanding what is challenging their full development and
the reason for those challenges. And this requires examining
the *mother* of those fears and anxieties—the real underlying
causes of them.

---

[33] Whyte, D. (1994). *The Heart Aroused.* New York: Currency
Doubleday, pp. 38-39.

Why Do We Fear?

Like the emperor, many of us are afraid to admit that we are a work-in-progress and that we have areas we need to develop.  Rather, we need to be proud that we have "growing edges" that need to be developed and honed, for we are modeling continual growth and development for our followers, co-workers, and even our bosses.  When we are able to enthusiastically demonstrate this, we give them permission to grow and develop as well.

Ken Wilber, a philosopher whose approach to philosophy integrates body, mind, soul, and Spirit with self, culture, and nature, believes that each of us must not merely see our realities anew (or, to use his words, the ***translation*** of our current understanding to a new belief or paradigm), but that we must be willing to undergo a complete ***transformation*** of ourselves.  In order to do this, Wilber believes that we must first shatter the Self—i.e., the ideas that we currently hold about ourselves and our abilities, gifts, and fears—and admit that these challenging aspects stem from our current view of the world, our role in it, and our

connection to others.  He explains the difference between

translation and transformation in this way:

> *With translation, the self is simply given a new way to think or feel about reality.  The self is given a new belief—perhaps holistic instead of atomistic, perhaps forgiveness instead of blame, perhaps relational instead of analytic.  The self then learns to translate its world and its being in the terms of this new belief or new language or new paradigm, and this new and enchanting translation acts, at least temporarily, to alleviate or diminish the terror inherent in the heart of the separate self.*
>
> *But with transformation, the very process of translation itself is challenged, witnessed, undermined, and eventually dismantled.  With typical translation, the self (or subject) is given a new way to think about the world (or objects); but with radical transformation, the self itself is inquired into, looked into, grabbed by its throat and literally throttled to death.*[34]

---

[34] Wilber, K. (1997). *The Eye of the Spirit*. Shambahala Publications, Inc., pp. 196-198.

94

Consider the translation of any current social issue: gay marriage, universal health care, climate change, or racism. Over time, society has "translated" these issues for many of us as rights and responsibilities to ourselves as a community. For example, a "translation" may be that climate change should be viewed as a body of scientific evidence of human failure rather than a social responsibility for future generations; or racism should be "translated" as a need for reparation, rather than as an apportionment of blame.

Individuals, however, have had to wrestle with their own values and beliefs in profound ways in order to arrive at their own understanding of issues and, in many cases, to completely transform how they see themselves as a part of the greater human community and, more importantly, their role in the creation and continuation of issues that affect the community of which they are a part—in our case, an organization, a department, a team, or a manager-employee relationship.

It is in this transformation that we feel our most vulnerable to criticism, challenging the very essence of who we thought we were. We feel some very real and primal fears and anxieties, like those represented by loss of control or disapproval from others. These fears are often at the root of our struggles when we consider taking on new roles and demonstrating our true potential.

Recognize that deep-seated needs, fears, and anxieties influence your Chuck's personal and professional lives. We have already intimated that need for control and need for approval stem from early life experiences, many of which flow from parental and peer relationships. However, *when anxieties and fears dominate behavior, they become problematic for establishing credibility and, thus, trustworthiness with others.*

Chuck's lack of credibility and untrustworthiness are ultimately his biggest problems for you, whether you are his boss, his peer, or his direct report. So, let's take a more in-depth look at trust and, specifically, how needs for approval and control jeopardize the trustworthiness we all need from our organizational colleagues.

# CHAPTER 6

## THE IMPORTANCE OF TRUST

## AND TRUSTWORTHINESS

*Three things are the sign of a hypocrite: when he speaks he tells lies, when he promises he breaks it, and when he is trusted he proves to be dishonest.*
—Islamic prophet, Muhammad, 570 CE – 632 CE

In the *Republic*, Plato says that things will go well only when those who govern the state do not desire to govern. In other words, people who want to be in leadership roles are automatically suspect with regard to their intentions. The 19th century philosopher, Søren Kierkegaard, seems to agree:

> *Assuming the necessary capability, a man's reluctance to govern affords a good guarantee that he will govern well and efficiently; whereas a man desirous of governing may very easily either abuse his power and become a tyrant, or by his desire to govern be brought into an unforeseen situation of*

*dependence on the people he is to rule, so that his government really becomes an illusion.*[35]

One implication of these reflections is that unless leaders minimize their needs for control and approval, and their followers believe that they have truly done so, their motives for leadership are likely to be questioned, even if they make decisions or take actions that may appear beneficent.  Or, as T.S. Eliot, in his work *Murder in the Cathedral*, put it, *The last temptation is the greatest treason: to do the right deed for the wrong reason.*  Once motives are questioned, the erosion of trust by followers begins.

Many scholars and theologians have written about the fundamental importance of trustworthiness in creating sustainable organizations and societies.  For example, James Clawson and Michael Blank found that trust and respect accounted for a full 75% of the amount of learning and

---

[35] Kierkegaard, S. (2010). *The Present Age: On the Death of Rebellion.* New York: Harper Perennial Modern Classics (originally published 1846).

openness of the subordinate to influence from his or her leader.[36]

In the Bahá'í tradition this quotation from an early 4th century Persian tablet is most illuminating about the role of trustworthiness:

> *Trustworthiness is the greatest portal leading unto the tranquility and security of the people. In truth, the stability of every affair hath depended and doth depend upon it. All the domains of power, of grandeur, and of wealth are illumined by its light.[37]*

This statement is true in all organizational settings. Trustworthy leaders, co-workers, and followers become more secure in the tasks required of them and, in return, their loyalty and diligence provide stability for their organizations and civil societies. As Russell Hardin puts it, "The best

---

[36] Clawson, J.G. and Blank, M.B. (1990). What really counts in superior subordinate relationships. *Mentoring International*, 4, 1, pp. 12-17.
[37] From the Fourth Taraz, gleaned from the Tablets of Baha'u'llah Revealed after the Kitab-i-Aqdas", p. 37

device for creating trust is to establish and support trustworthiness."[38]

When we attain trustworthiness in the eyes of others, only then can we begin to create a sustainable organization or an enduring society capable of great things. That said, **trustworthiness might be the single most important factor in establishing and maintaining an authentic relationship with others**.

But what does it mean to trust and to be trusted? How can people feel secure enough to put their welfare into the hands of others? There are several ways to understand the notion of trust: as encapsulated interest, as a cost-benefit calculus, and as interpersonal identification.

Trust as Encapsulated Interest

Political scientist Russell Hardin believes that much of what we call trust can be best described as *encapsulated interest*. Hardin would argue that we place our trust in those

---

[38] Hardin, R. (1996). Trustworthiness. *Ethics*, 107, pp. 26-42.

whom we believe to have strong reasons to act in our best interests. He writes,

> *It is this fact that makes my trust more than merely expectations about your behavior. Any expectations I have are grounded in an understanding (perhaps mistaken) of your interests specifically with respect to me.*[39]

The "Encapsulated Interest" view implies that anyone whose interests are supposedly aligned with ours deserves our trust. Unfortunately, this perspective is not always accurate, as evidenced by the rash of corporate and political scandals that continue to plague the world. In these all-too-blatant instances of betrayal of trust, leaders say one thing and do another.

Think about your Chuck. You likely evaluate how her actions will affect you, first and foremost, by what she says. Then, after she has acted, you probably evaluate whether or not Chuck did what she said she would do. If so,

---

[39] Hardin, R. (2002). *Trust and trustworthiness*. New York: Russell Sage Foundation, p.2.

you are likely to have increasing confidence in what Chuck says in the future and to trust that she will act similarly as she has in the past. Over time, Chuck will become increasingly trustworthy if her actions are consistent with what she ultimately says and does. Of course, consistency with word and deed can also result in negative actions (e.g., "I said I would lay off 20% of the workforce, and I did"); from a trust perspective, however, Chuck's actions <u>are</u> consistent with her words, so you would likely believe her when she threatens layoffs in the future.

The bottom line is that to place trust in our leaders and colleagues, we must see them as trustworthy. No matter how often they espouse their interests to be in line with our own (e.g., liberty and freedom, increased number of jobs, improved social conditions, organizational profitability, eradication of disease and poverty, etc.) we have difficulty believing untrustworthy people, primarily because their *behavior* differs so greatly from their *words*. We *hear* their stated positions, but we *see* budgets, policies, outsourcing, and removal or denial of liberties that don't support those positions. In sum, we begin to be distrustful of people when their words don't match their actions and when their interests and our interests appear incompatible.

## Trust as a Cost-Benefit Calculus

Another view of trust is as a sort of *calculus* by which an individual is assumed to calculate the benefits of being in relationship with another person versus the costs of not being in relationship. In this view, trust will only be extended to another to the extent that the cost-benefit calculation indicates that an ongoing relationship with someone will yield a net positive benefit for the individual. Or, to put it another way, "I will trust you only if I believe that I will gain because of extending that trust to you," or "I will not trust you if I believe that the costs of extending that trust to you outweighs the benefits I will gain by doing so."

This view of trust is also grounded in one's judgments about whether the other person will behave predictably and reliably. Sometimes these judgments are flawed and based on false assumptions.[40] Similar to the encapsulated interest model, we determine whether we will trust someone based on the predicted outcomes for us—in this case, a continuing relationship.

It is also true that minor trust violations may result in reducing one's level of trust in one situation, but not another. For example, you may trust your Chuck to not reveal to coworkers that you are contemplating a divorce, but not trust him to make the decision to report one of his close peers for falsifying an expense report. As a result, because we have to continue to interact or work with Chuck, the relationship becomes superficial and our behavior highly self-monitored.

Both the Encapsulated Interest and Calculus views are quite self-centered: we tend to extend trust to those who will benefit our interests or who will not harm us. Usually people holding either of these views are more concerned with

[40] Lewicki, R.J. and Tomlinson, E.C. (2003). Trust and trust building. *Beyond Intractability*. Eds., Guy Burgess and Heidi Burgess. Conflict Research Consortium, University of Colorado, Boulder.

how another's actions affect them personally and immediately, rather than the effect of their actions on the greater good for an organization in the long-term.

For example, let's say that you distrust Chuck, the CEO of your organization, because he has begun outsourcing jobs to India. Are you focusing on the effect of that decision on your own individual job and livelihood? Are you ignoring more "big picture" outcomes, such as the broadening of economic markets (e.g., India) that should produce future demand for more (not fewer) products and a greater (not a lesser) need for U.S. talent as a result? Obviously, CEOs are in positions in which they are required to determine the effect of their actions in broader, more encompassing ways. Judging whether someone is a trustworthy requires us to look at the totality and sustainability of their decisions and behaviors on all stakeholders, not merely on the effect they have on any one individual or group during a finite and limited period of time.

A good example of this is a political leader. Political leaders often focus on their immediate constituencies, particularly during election times. Federal representatives from farm states make a big effort to show the number of times they voted for legislation that would benefit farmers, while those from industrial states emphasize their concern and support for manufacturing concerns. But the true test for the sustainable benefits of their decisions comes much later than a November election. In fact, history is replete with examples of "political" decisions that ultimately benefited no one but a politician's re-election campaign.

When deciding whether or not Chuck is trustworthy, we mentally assign a measure of "trustworthiness" to her, based on how consistently, reliably, and equitably she has acted over time. Therefore, it is unlikely that Chuck will be trusted until she has demonstrated consistent and fair behavior across different situations with many different people.

## Trust as Interpersonal Identification

Social scientists see trust and trustworthiness as more complex than calculations based merely on an alignment of interests or accrued benefits for individuals. For starters, we may perceive someone as trustworthy, but not actually act on that perception. This subtle distinction is the difference between making a relatively impersonal evaluation of another and our active investment in outcomes of relevant importance to us.[41] In other words, we can *say* that we trust someone, but until we *act* as if we do, followed by our evaluation of the outcomes stemming from those actions, we cannot know if our trust in that person was warranted.

This implies that we can only assess someone's trustworthiness retrospectively. Thus, ***the decision to trust another is based on our past experiences with them, but the actual feeling of trust is geared to our future behavior***. Those individuals with whom we have ongoing and valuable

---

[41] Tanis, M. and Postmes, T. (2005). A social identity approach to trust: Interpersonal perception, group membership, and trusting behavior. *European Journal of Social Psychology*, 35, pp.413-424.

relationships are more likely to garner our trust in the future than people who are merely acquaintances or with whom we have limited experience, just like the fox in the story of *The Little Prince*:

> *"What must I do to tame you?" asked the little prince.*
>
> *"You must be very patient," replied the fox. "First you will sit down at a little distance from me—like that—in the grass. I shall look at you out of the corner of my eye, and you will say nothing. Words are the source of misunderstandings. But you will sit a little closer to me, every day...."* [42]

This idea is supported by research suggesting that trust builds in stages, growing stronger and more resilient, and it changes in character.[43] That is, as a relationship grows through deeper understanding and repeated interactions, the individuals involved may become increasingly aware of shared values and goals. This allows trust to grow to a

---

[42] de Saint-Exupéry, Antoine Marie Roger (1943). *The Little Prince,* Harcourt Brace Jovanovich, Inc.
[43] See, for example, Lewicki, R. J., McAllister, D. J., & Bies, R. J. (1998). Trust and distrust: New relationships and realities. *Academy of Management Review, 23,* pp. 438-458.

higher and qualitatively different level and begin to be a transforming experience for the relationship itself.

When trust evolves to the highest level, it is said to function as *identification-based* trust. At this point, trust has been built to the point that the parties involved have internalized each other's desires and intentions. They understand what the other party really cares about so completely that each party is able to act for the other. At this advanced stage, trust is also enhanced by a strong emotional bond between the parties, based on a sense of shared goals and values. They know that only the most grievous of behaviors can disrupt the bond between them, creating the feeling that no separation truly exists between them. So this view of trust, as a more emotionally-driven phenomenon, is grounded in perceptions of interpersonal care and concern.

## Trust and Risk-taking

At this level of trust and trustworthiness, the beliefs held by one person about another's intentions, abilities, and integrity may lead them to take risks in their relationship with that person by sharing information, taking on responsibilities, working together on tasks, etc. Self-disclosure, for example, is an example of a behavior that requires risk-taking on the part of the person sharing information. That is, we generally don't self-disclose private thoughts and feelings to people we don't fully trust. Otherwise, we feel vulnerable, having given up some of our control to someone else and risking their disapproval of us.

As individuals, we have differing views on how to approach trusting others. For example, some of us start off trusting people and stop only if they prove that they are not trustworthy. Others are initially cautious, preferring not to trust until the other person proves to be trustworthy. Of course, there is no "right" or "wrong" way to approach the matter of trust; but it is worth remembering that each of us approaches this process differently, based on our own past experiences and comfort levels.

We also tend to trust others when we believe that they are still willing to learn and develop. This allows us to respect them and to treat them as we would ourselves, because we can see that they are aware of their own humanity, with all its pitfalls and frailties. It is seeing each other truthfully and authentically—not as heroes and geniuses, but as the recipients of responsible care and concern for others—that allows our trust to grow.

This becomes important for leaders to understand, particularly those who are beginning new relationships with followers. Take, for example, Jim, who was a close friend to several people at work prior to being promoted and becoming their leader. Their relationship as peers was based on relative equality regarding pay, authority, control, and other aspects of their work lives. But, when Jim was promoted into a leadership role, the relationship he had with his peers changed to one of less trust—even though he hadn't done anything differently or "untrustworthy" to warrant that change. Jim's peers merely awarded "trustworthiness" differently to peers than they did to their leaders, primarily because of their perception of risk in being vulnerable to their leaders. They typically trusted peers and only stopped trusting them if the peers proved untrustworthy; however, with leaders they were more cautious, withholding trust until the leaders proved trustworthy.

Amazing, isn't it? Even though Jim was the same person, his role as "leader" automatically made him less trustworthy among his former peers. And that is why Jim, the Leader, has to work to build the trust that Jim, the Peer, already had, because many followers assume that leaders, overall, do not share the same values and goals, cares and concerns that they do.

We attain trustworthy status by demonstrating that we are not substantively different from our bosses, peers, and direct reports, particularly in the values they hold dear. Because trustworthiness requires an emotional connection to achieve, becoming a "trustworthy Chuck" means recognizing the bond that connects us with our colleagues, our customers, and our communities. To attain trustworthiness in the eyes of another, then, one must believe and act upon that premise; to do otherwise, is to create mistrust, hostility, and separation.


## What Do Approval and Control Have to Do With Trust?

But what keeps us from trusting others and acting trustworthy ourselves, if we buy into the premise that we are connected to each other? What prevents us from seeing the similarities, rather than the differences, we share? Once again, our approval and control needs are creating the fear that distorts our views of each other and ourselves. These needs prevent us from becoming a trusting and trustworthy manager, peer, or co-worker.

First and foremost, *trusting behavior requires that we relinquish complete control over processes and outcomes that are important to us.* In order to develop trustworthiness, we must be willing to be vulnerable and humble. It is scary to be vulnerable and, to some people, humility is a sign of weakness. As we have discussed previously, the difficulty most people have in giving up control is that they become vulnerable to rejection and criticism. They are afraid to "let go," because they may end up responsible and accountable for their own mistakes and judgment, as well as for others' incorrect decisions.

Many of you may have experienced this with your "Chuck." Does your Chuck typically micromanage your projects or refuse to delegate work to anyone? Does he or she tend to blame others or, at least, refuse to take blame for poor outcomes of decisions? If these sound familiar, it is likely that your Chuck also has a high need for control. Your Chuck may also have a problem trusting others and, perhaps, is perceived untrustworthy by you and your colleagues.

Sometimes Chucks also tend to avoid full emotional involvement with others by concealing their mistakes or distrusting others to do tasks. In this, they become vulnerable to their own *lack of trust in self*, which is rooted in a deep need for approval. If Chuck doesn't trust herself, this is likely at the very heart of not being able to trust others.

This poem by Nyoshul Khenpo speaks to the ability for all of

us to see how our lack of self-trust develops:

## Autobiography in Five Chapters[44]

### Chapter I
*I walk down the street.*
*There is a deep hole in the sidewalk.*
*I fall in.*
*I am lost...I am hopeless.*
*It isn't my fault.*
*It takes forever to find a way out.*

### Chapter II
*I walk down the same street.*
*There is a deep hole in the sidewalk.*
*I pretend I don't see it.*
*I fall in again.*
*I can't believe I'm in the same place, but it isn't my fault.*
*It still takes a long time to get out.*

### Chapter III
*I walk down the same street.*
*There is a deep hole in the sidewalk.*
*I see it is there.*
*I still fall in...it's a habit.*
*My eyes are open.*
*I know where I am.*
*It is my fault.*
*I get out immediately.*

---

[44] Khenpo, N. Autobiography in five chapters. Reprinted in Sogyal Rinpoche, *The Tibetan Book of Living and Dying.*

***Chapter IV***
*I walk down the same street.*
*There is a deep hole in the sidewalk.*
*I walk around it.*

***Chapter V***
*I walk down another street.*


Part of developing our self-trust is to realize we have choices

to continue the way we have always behaved or to change

how we see ourselves and, thus, to do something concrete

about it—to "walk down another street," as it were.

Determining whether to trust others causes us to look

for behaviors they exhibit that we approve of.  Therefore,

when we see behavior that doesn't fit our model of what a

trustworthy person should do, we withhold trust until we

observe different behavior that supports our model.  We only

begin to trust when we see behavior that, over time,

confirms, rather than disconfirms, what we approve of.

## Becoming More Trustworthy

So, what influences how trustworthy we appear to others or they appear to us? Three important questions provide clues:

- *Am I acting authentically?* Am I acting in a manner that is consistent with who I say and believe that I am? People who do not "walk the talk" and do not appear to be who they say they are will never gain the trust of others. It is often the "unauthentic" behaviors of Chuck that undermines our trust of him.

- *Can I really do what I say I can do?* Am I competent in those things in which I profess to be competent? When we do not appear competent we will not gain trust, no matter what else we do or how much integrity we appear to possess.

- *Will I really do what I say I will do?* Is my actual behavior reliable and consistent with my promised behavior? People who say one thing and do quite another are usually perceived as untrustworthy.

However, there is one exception to this: if what prevented someone from doing what she said she would do is perceived to be a legitimate reason. However, she will be put on a very short leash after such an event; that is, her peers, subordinates, or boss may allow it once, but that's about it.

Research has shown us that leaders who lack trust from followers tend to be angry, competitive, resentful, and lack empathy,[45] while leaders who are trustworthy tend to be happier, better liked by others, more honest, and more moralistic.[46] Trustworthy leaders do what they say they will do, and they never betray the confidence of those who trust them. To see where you currently stand on your own trustworthiness as a leader, take the *"Are You a Trustworthy Leader?"* quiz at the end of this chapter. Additionally, try

---

[45] Gurtman, MB 1992. Trust, distrust, and interpersonal problems: A circumplex analysis. *Journal of Personality and Social Psychology*, 62 (6), pp.989-1002.
[46] Rotter, J.B. 1980. Interpersonal trust, trustworthiness, and gullibility. *American Psychologist*, 35, 1, pp. 1-7.

giving it to someone who knows you well and see if that person agrees with you.

If gaining trust is determined largely by authenticity, competency, and the consistency and reliability of behavior, then how should this be demonstrated to others? What types of behaviors can we demonstrate that show others that we, indeed, are trusting *and* trustworthy? Here are a few suggestions:

- ***Let others know your feelings, emotions, and reactions***; do not hide them because of fear, particularly of losing approval from others. These aspects of the real you are what forge the bonds of relationships. No one fully trusts those with whom they do not have a deep connection.

- ***Place confidence in others*** so that they will be supportive and reinforcing of you, even if you let down your "strong" mask and show your weaknesses. It's important for you to talk about your difficulties and mistakes from time to time. It makes you seem more human.

- ***Assume that others will not intentionally hurt or abuse you***, should you make an error or a mistake. Otherwise, you will eventually become reclusive, isolated, and distrustful.

- ***Let others into your life*** so that you and they can create a relationship built on an understanding of mutual respect, caring, and concern to assist one another in growing and maturing independently.

- ***Rely on others to treat you in a fair, open, and honest way***. If people act fairly and honestly, they will eventually experience similar behavior.

- ***Do not act like a "victim."*** You are in control of your choices, even if the consequences of your choices are not what you wanted or expected.

- ***Create a healing environment*** around you. Participate actively in forgiveness, understanding, and healthy communication to resolve problems and issues. Avoid blaming others; rather, encourage them to talk about their mistakes, just as you do.

- *Accept who you are* in the present moment. This is the real you, anyway.

As you begin to act trustworthy and to gain the trust of your peers, your followers, and your boss, you will be able to start the work of helping others to learn, grow, and change. As a result, you will be given more trust, responsibility, and influence in shaping the organizations you work for.

---

**EXERCISE—Discovering Causes for Distrust**
If you have issues with trusting others or being perceived as untrustworthy, answer these questions to find out why, and then determine which behaviors or beliefs you need to develop:

1. Am I lacking trust in persons, groups, or institutions? If yes, in which persons, groups, or institutions do I lack trust? How does this lack of trust manifest itself?
2. Why do I lack trust in the persons, groups, or institutions listed above? What is the role of my need for approval or need for control in creating my lack of trust?
3. What beliefs do I hold that underlie my lack of trust in the persons, groups, or institutions listed?
4. What new information, beliefs, perceptions, or attitudes do I need to acquire or develop in order to have more trust in the persons, groups, or institutions listed?

## What's Next?

In the next section, we will look more closely at the underpinnings of several challenges we talked about earlier that have need for control and need for approval underpinnings. For the first of these—Lack of Emotional Control—we begin by looking at the role of the human brain.

# ARE YOU A TRUSTWORTHY LEADER?[47]

*Answer these questions as honestly as you can. If you have never been in a leadership role, ask someone else who knows you well to evaluate what they think you would do, based on their experiences with you to date.*

1. Your company has recently sold a product line that will result in transfers, job reassignments, and possible layoffs for your group. In making these personnel decisions, will you:

    ○ A. Go to extremes to be fair and do the right thing, even if this is counter to the "company line"

    ○ B. Set up an evaluation process for everyone, except personal friends

    ○ C. Do what is politically correct and pleasing to top management

2. Customer demands require that one person in your department works on Christmas day. Will you:

    ○ A. Decide who will work based on who has the lowest seniority in the department

    ○ B. Offer to work unless someone else needs to work that day

    ○ C. Set up a rotation where everyone in the department, including you, the leader, will take a turn working this holiday

3. You have committed to helping your staff keep life and work in better balance by being more realistic in setting goals, priorities, and deadlines. What's the best statement about your behavior?

---

[47] Adapted from *Training & Development*, December 1997, pp. 11.

○ A. I will put forth a good effort but, with time, start to make exceptions

○ B. Sounds good, but the next time upper management and/or the client puts the heat on it will be back to "crunch" time and business as usual

○ C. Regardless of what happens, I will honor my commitments.

4. One of your employees received a lower performance evaluation and salary increase than expected. When they ask you to explain, you will:

○ A. Be forthright, honest, and truthful with the explanation

○ B. Be uncomfortable and tell only part of the reasons

○ C. Explain how you did not have full control over the decision

5. Having just attended a farewell lunch for a close associate, one of your staff returns to the office and is called for a random drug test. The two glasses of wine punch at lunch (no surprise) leads to a small amount of alcohol detected. Will you:

○ A. Strictly adhere to company policy and put the staff member on a leave of absence

○ B. After a discussion, realize that this is a unique situation, exercise good judgment, and ignore the test

○ C. Recommend that the person enroll in the company's employee assistance counseling program

6. The first formal presentation of a junior staff member to the top management committee isn't going well at all. Will you, as her leader:

    ○  A. Jump in and ask for the presentation to be reschedule so "she can be better prepared"

    ○  B. Let her sink, and ask embarrassing questions, knowing that this is how lasting lessons are learned

    ○  C. Jump in to protect, support, and encourage her in a way that allows her to save face

7. There are rumors floating around about a significant change in direction and reorganization for your department. When asked by your staff, you:

    ○  A. Can be counted on to freely share all the information and ideas available

    ○  B. Will tell only what you think they need to know

    ○  C. Will discuss the changes only after they have been announced

8. You have been observed as a leader in a variety of situations. How would your staff describe what your behavior will be in an upcoming critical client meeting?

    ○  A. They haven't a clue, each day is a new day with you

    ○  B. Very predictable, there is little doubt in their mind how you will behave in various situations

    ○  C. Since this is a new client, they think they know how you will behave, but they are less than 60% sure of their predictions

9. Having known and worked with you for a number of years, would your staff say:

    ○ A. Your record is sporadic; sometimes you could be trusted, sometimes not

    ○ B. Knowing what they know about you, there is no way they would trust you

    ○ C. History indicates that you can be trusted implicitly

10. A decision needs to be made that will have a huge impact on the direction of your department. Will you:

    ○ A. Respect and treat each person as an equal partner in making this decision

    ○ B. Consult with and listen to others' input then make the decision yourself

    ○ C. As the boss, analyze the facts in the situation, seek little input, and then make the decision you think is best

## Scoring

1. A=10, B=5, C=2 — Implementing and abiding by procedures that treat everyone fairly will increase the trust others have in you. Not showing favorites and being willing to take a stand for fairness are critical elements of this dimension of trust.

2. A=2, B=10, C=5 — How concerned are you with the goodwill and interests of others? Actions that place their self-interests before yours are strong indicators of your genuine concern and sensitivity to their self interests.

3. A=5, B=2, C=10 — Can you be counted on to keep your commitments in both the good and bad times? You can't trust someone who says one thing and does the other or when pressured, conveniently forgets commitments.

4. A=10, B=5, C=2 — How would others rate your integrity? Two key elements in their conclusions would be your reputation for honesty and truthfulness even when this might be uncomfortable. How could others trust someone who is dishonest or tells only half-truths?

5. A=2, B=10, C=5 — Your consistency, reliability, predictability, and good judgment in handling situations will tell others that you can be trusted. Do you temper all of this with good judgment? Can you be counted on to "do what is right" even in the face of contradictory circumstances?

6. A=5, B=2, C=10 — Other's trust in you will increase if they see you as loyal and willing to protect, support and encourage them. Exhibiting caring compassion and running interference, allows you to experiment in an environment that is non-threatening to your self-image.

8. A=5, B=2, C=10 — Are you predictable, reliable, and responsive in a caring way? How can other trust

someone whose actions are random?

9. C=10, A=5, B=2

An indicator of how much trust others can place in you is your track record. History does repeat itself. Ask yourself if the evidence supports the case for others trusting you.

10. A=10, B=5, C=2

Trust is reciprocal. Through your words and actions, do you openly show others that you trust and respect them when it really counts? If you don't trust them, how can you expect them to trust you?

## Your score

80-100

Your actions are consistent regardless of the person, place, or event. You care for others, are consistent, do the right things regardless of personal risk, and exude integrity. Congratulations, others find working with you a unique and rewarding experience.

50-80

Your closest confidants can trust you, others are not sure—sometimes yes, sometimes no. The word is consistency. Seek out and change those actions that are sending mixed signals if you want higher levels of trust from others.

20-50

You probably find others become quiet when you walk in the room, seem to weigh their words, and begrudgingly share information with you. You often feel lonely, but the good news is that you can change. Look over the quiz and ask how you can start to behave in a more trustworthy fashion.

# CHAPTER 7

## The Challenge of Emotional Control

### *Challenge #1: Inability to Control Emotions*

*It is important to keep in mind that it is your own thoughts, bodily changes, and behaviors that drive your emotional responses, not someone else's actions or an event.*

– Hendrie D. Weisinger[48]

Before we talk about how to deal with specific challenges posed by a lack of emotional control, either your own or to respond to Chuck's, it may be helpful to understand how our brains work to regulate our emotions. Once you realize that emotions are largely an automatic function of the human brain, it is much easier to learn how to begin controlling them.

## It All Begins in the Brain!

Dr. Paul D. MacLean, a prominent brain researcher, developed a model of brain structure that he calls the "triune

---

[48] Weisinger, H.D. (1998) *Emotional Intelligence at Work.* San Francisco, CA: Jossey-Bass.

brain." In other words, humans have not one brain, but three interconnected biological computers, each having "its own special intelligence, its own subjectivity, its own sense of time and space, its own memory, motor, and other functions."[49] Each of the three brains corresponds to a major evolutionary development, categorized as follows: the reptilian brain or cerebellum (survival functions), the old mammalian brain or limbic system (emotional functions), and the new mammalian brain or neocortex (reasoning functions).

Human physiology has evolved over millions of years. From the time primordial sea creatures crawled onto land, the adaptation of their physical and mental abilities began. In human brains, the most ancient and smallest of the three brains evolved because of a need to survive under adverse conditions. This small brain is around 200 million years old and is referred to as the *reptilian brain*. Much of

---

[49] MacLean, P.D. (1993). "Evolution of Three Mentalities," *Brain, Culture, & the Human Spirit: Essays from an Emergent Evolutionary Perspective,* J.B. Ashbrook, Editor, Maryland: University Press of America, Inc., p. 24.

human behavior can be described in reptilian terms, especially those involving aggression and territoriality. It primarily regulates the "fight or flight" response, breathing, heart rate, and other autonomic functions.

The old mammalian brain, or the *limbic system*, is sandwiched between the reptilian brain and the new mammalian brain or neocortex. This brain evolved about 60 million years ago, over 100+ million years after the original reptilian brain. It is far more sensitive and sophisticated than the reptilian brain. The limbic system is concerned with the emotions, and it plays a different, but nevertheless major, role in aggression and fear. It is largely responsible for the resetting of various bodily systems during our emotional reactions. The limbic system also is thought to be the origin of altruistic, as well as sexual, behaviors.

The newest brain, the *neocortex* or new mammalian brain, only developed a few million years ago. In humans, the neocortex is also the largest of the three brains, accounting for about five-sixths of the entire human brain. It is responsible for higher-order thinking skills, reason, linguistic expression, and verbal memory. The job of the neocortex is to detect patterns and interpret the meanings of situations. In essence, it is this large, higher-order thinking part of our brain that distinguishes humans from other species.

Many of us make the mistake in assuming that events and circumstances directly *cause* our emotional states. But this is incorrect. Humans rely heavily on the neocortex to *interpret* events. However, sometimes we forget that the cognitive process of interpretation comes *between* the event and our emotional reaction to it.

**Figure 1    The Triune Brain and Its Functions**

| Reptilian Brain (Cerebellum) | Old Mammalian Brain (Limbic System) | New Mammalian Brain (Neocortex) |
|---|---|---|
| • "Fight" or "Flight" <br> • Automatic Thoughts | • Emotions <br> • Memories <br> • Sexual Response | • Language <br> • Rational Thought <br> • Imagination |

In many instances, emotional responses are directly preceded by automatic thoughts, that is, those thoughts that have developed over time based on previous experiences, conditioning, and so forth. They often arise from specific internal needs—such as the needs for approval or control—and from unresolved developmental conflicts from our childhood. For example, if we speak with someone and they start smiling, we might interpret that smile in one of two ways: either that they are laughing at us or that they could be pleased at something we said. If we have a history of being teased, and we let automatic thought prevail, we may interpret the smile as negative and believe the person is making fun of us. Our reaction, then, would be based on our negative perception and interpretation of the other person's behavior (their smile).

Automatic thoughts remain hidden beneath the surface for most people. They don't realize they are having them. When automatic thoughts control our emotional responses to people, problems, and events, we ignore evidence that contradicts the automatic thought. It is when we allow ourselves to be controlled by our survival or emotional brains—without feedback from the neocortex—that we run into problems. Unless we train ourselves to look for these thoughts, we will probably be unaware of them. Getting a handle on our emotions is a matter of gaining conscious control over those thoughts that occur automatically. Emotional control is essentially a matter of detaching ourselves from our negative emotions that are brought on by self-defeating automatic thoughts.

This probably happens when Chuck's survival programming prods him to lash out at someone who he feels is challenging his position in a business meeting. If he were to pause and consciously consider the situation, he would probably come up with a much more effective strategy or course of action. But, as long as Chuck continues to think and behave automatically, it is his survival programming that is running the show, not his reasoning function.

Of course, the whole idea behind developing healthy emotional control is that *the person is the one in control*, not his automatic programming or emotions. Without developing an ability to control emotions, Chuck will always be challenged by his behavior and, ultimately, gaining the trust of others. In reality, this ability requires continual development in most people.

In *The Fifth Discipline*, Peter M. Senge quotes an article called "Advanced Maturity," written by Bill O'Brien, and it is worth reproducing here:

> *Whatever the reasons, we do not pursue emotional development with the same intensity with which we pursue physical and intellectual development. This is all the more unfortunate, because full emotional development offers the greatest degree of leverage in attaining our full potential.*[50]

That said, two areas of emotional control seem to be the most prominent areas of challenge for the "Chucks" we work with—impatience and anger.

---

[50] Senge, P. (2006). *The Fifth Discipline: The Art and Practice of the Learning Organization.* NY: Doubleday, p. 133.

## Impatience

> *Patience is a hard discipline. It is not just waiting until something happens over which we have no control: the arrival of the bus, the end of the rain, the return of a friend, the resolution of a conflict. Patience is not a waiting passivity until someone else does something. Patience asks us to live the moment to the fullest, to be completely present to the moment, to taste the here and now, to be where we are. When we are impatient, we try to get away from where we are. We behave as if the real thing will happen tomorrow, later, and somewhere else. Be patient and trust that the treasure you are looking for is hidden in the ground on which you stand.*
>
> —Henri J. M. Nouwen, theologian

Patience is having the power of *acceptance*, i.e., acceptance of people as they are in that moment and acceptance of events as they are happening. To be present in the moment, and to accept where we are at that moment, is to be aware that something better may be in front of us. Or, at least, we often hope that is the case. Particularly in Western cultures, we are encouraged as children, as students, and as leaders to be focused on future goals and destinations; our frustration (and, thus, our impatience) comes from the desire to always be moving forward, to be in progress toward something more desirable and beneficial. As a friend of mine once confessed, "I hate being stuck in traffic at a standstill. Even if I'm at least crawling along, I feel better." Many of us feel better if we're working toward something and moving forward, at least a bit. Though, as Nouwen suggests, we are moving away from where we are, despite the fact that the place where we are at that moment may be the best place for us. And, for many of us, we have difficulty being patient with ourselves, because we have experienced impatience from family, teachers, and friends over our lifetimes. Again, our automatic thoughts are at work.

Stephen Covey writes that much of our impatience stems from emotional immaturity: *In our quest to become better leaders, we become enslaved by emotions, particularly anger and impatience.* [51]  Impatience makes us want to get to the end of the journey without actually taking the journey.

People who suffer from severe impatience are often considered to be arrogant, insensitive, and overbearing. Impatience also manifests itself in abrupt behaviors, such as cutting others off in mid-sentence and making what appear to be uninformed, quick judgments. The impatient person may snap at others in response to questions or requests, or may just take over a task, frustrated by the process used or how slowly others take to do it. Interestingly, most people generally know that they suffer from impatience, but controlling their impatience depends a great deal on learning why they experience it and what triggers it.

Impatience likely has control underpinnings. That is, we may act impatiently when we are frustrated by our inability to gain or maintain control of a person, situation, task, process, or outcome. We believe that it is all up to us and, as a consequence, we experience frustration with others

---

[51] Covey, S.R. (1990) *Principle-Centered Leadership.* New York: Fireside.

when they don't do things quickly enough or well enough to meet our expectations. Consider an excerpt from one new leader's analysis who described her impatience this way:

> *I am an incredibly busy person and time constraints are often an issue in my everyday life. Therefore, I become impatient when I feel that additional time is being consumed where it is not needed. Frequently, I find myself overlooking the fact that people may not have the knowledge or skills to quickly complete a task. For instance, when training people at my job, I repeatedly find myself growing uncontrollably irritated when the trainee takes added time to perform a task that would have taken me a fraction of the time. Furthermore, when speaking with people, I would rather they get to the main point instead of wasting my time with meaningless details.*

Part of the impatience she feels may be linked to feelings of superiority on her part. Put another way, she is not necessarily attentive to people who she believes do not have information of value to her. In some ways, this is self-centered and controlling. If she is encouraged to think about her view of others in relationship to her view of herself, this may help her to realize that everyone has value, and it is up to her to identify the gifts others bring to the party. Moreover, the ability to invest time in making sure an employee (1) understands expectations and the importance of the task outcome or process, (2) has the adequate knowledge, skills, and time to practice them, and (3) knows the points in a project where decisions will have to be made can go a long way in helping her to trust that the work will get done correctly (and may save her more time in the long run).

Although impatience may stem from a high need to control people or situations, sometimes, impatience is the result of our inability to communicate what we really want or need. The irony with impatience is that we often focus on the shortcomings of others or on the confines of situations, when it is really our own needs that are not being met to our satisfaction. Our inability or unwillingness to give voice to these desires perpetuates the impatient behavior.

These latter aspects of an impatient nature are based on a need for approval. One's struggle to feel as if he or she is "good enough" often sets up a need for *more*: more time to finish a task, more positive strokes, more information to make a good decision, or more perfection. Though, as these lines from Johanna Atman's poem suggest, impatience often masks this underlying need for approval by posing as frustration with others and situations:

### *Impatience!*

*Alone, Impatience gulps black tea, and*

*Binges on information in such continuous undigested*

*portions,*

*it does not nourish her.*

*Her psyche bloated, an unseen leak*

*Leaves her never satisfied.*

*Usually with her sister, Frustration,*

*who tells her what to do,*

*they hang out with Fear of not enough:*

*not enough time, not enough done, not enough love.*

*With shallow breaths and busyness,*

*In collusion keep from ever arising,*

*The feeling of not being enough.*[52]

Conversely, patience allows us to listen more closely and attentively, to gather better information, and to take the time to make more informed, careful decisions. As the Dutch proverb says, *"A handful of patience is worth more than a bushel of brains."*

Anger

Anger is an unpleasant emotional state characterized by high physiological arousal. The pulse quickens, respiration increases, the pupils of the eyes constrict, blood rushes to the striated muscles of the body (the muscles that move the body's bones), and the adrenal glands pump out hormones. From the primitive biological point of view (our reptilian brain programming), the angry person is demonstrating the response pattern known as the *fight-or-*

---

[52] Excerpted from *Impatience!* by Johanna Atman, http://harbingerproject.com/issue35/impatience.htm

*flight reaction.* If the angered person has no appropriate coping mechanism (i.e., to confront what is angering him or her or to avoid it), the anger can become *latent anger*, which is then repressed at an unconscious level, only to emerge at some point in a chronic, pathological response. Chronic latent anger presents a real problem, mainly because it is *pathological, excessive, and irrational.* It may even contribute to physical problems over time, such as cardiovascular disease.[53]

Some of the signs and symptoms of anger merit comment. *Impatience* and *constant hurrying* are both aspects of a general attitude that is called *time urgency.* It is as if the chronically angry person is in a pressure cooker. We have already dealt previously with the issue of impatience, and it isn't difficult to see that impatience and anger can stem from similar origins.

---

[53] Chang, P. et al (2002). Anger in young men and subsequent premature cardiovascular disease: The precursors study, *Archives of Internal Medicine*, Apr. 22nd.

*Free-floating hostility* is characterized by being mad at everybody and everything. The chronically angry person is ready to hurl negative psychological thunderbolts at the slightest provocation. Thus, others are constantly discounted, abused, or even insulted. Privately, people are given such labels as stupid, incompetent, and lazy. Instead of recognizing that anger arises from within, the angry person sees external things and people as its source.

This symptom of anger is a bit more complex, having its roots in early childhood experiences that led the person to see the world as unsafe and threatening. Chronic anger may be, at its core, a defense against emotional insecurity. If a child grows up in a family that expresses frequent, irrational outbursts of anger, then observational learning can play a role in a tendency toward chronic anger. The person may imitate the behavior of parents or older siblings, since he or she was given tacit permission as a child to express aggressive impulses without sufficient restraint. It is also possible that the chronic anger took the form of verbally or physically bullying others as a child or adolescent. This intimidation continues because of the short-term psychological payoffs that reinforce the angry person's feelings of control and power. In this way, anger can be considered one's need to control turned inside out.

The *frustration-aggression hypothesis* states that aggression is a natural response to frustration. Frustration occurs when an individual is unable (1) to attain a desirable goal or (2) to escape from, or avoid, an unpleasant situation. Thus, chronic anger may result when a person believes, correctly or incorrectly, that life presents a constant stream of frustrating events. Like the power of a dammed river, aggression and anger can burst forth once the frustration becomes overwhelming.

## LEARNING TO CONTROL EMOTIONS

As many of us have discovered already, an inability to control one's emotions is an important, and potentially career-ending, challenge. This inability is our old reptilian brains or our limbic systems taking over our reasoning brain. Daniel Goleman, as well as a number of other researchers, has argued that leaders fail most often because of their inability to manage their emotions and moods, as well as their inability to empathize and get along with others.[54] In other words, a "Chuck's" *emotional intelligence* is more predictive of his or her success in relating to others (e.g., bosses, peers, direct reports, customers) than many other personality or behavioral predictors.

The two emotional challenges we've discussed here—impatience and anger—are only two of a wide range of emotional responses. But, they are two of the most costly. Here is one way to get a handle on these types of challenges if you have them.

- ***Discover the validity of "automatic thoughts" that precede your impatience or anger*** by keeping a record for two weeks. Write down what event or situation prompted the thought,

---

[54] Goleman, D. (1995). *Emotional Intelligence* (New York: Bantam Books.

your thoughts immediately following, the emotion

you felt about it, and what you actually did

(behavior). You could use a form that looks

something like this:

| Event | Emotions | Automatic Thoughts | Logical Comebacks |
|-------|----------|--------------------|--------------------|
|       |          |                    |                    |
|       |          |                    |                    |
|       |          |                    |                    |

The *Event* is a factual description with no emotions

attached. For example, you might say, "Clothes shopping

with my sister," rather than "Sister acting like she knows

everything I should buy on a shopping trip." The latter

statement contains your interpretation of the event, which

would be more properly listed in the "automatic thoughts"

column.

Your *Emotions* describe how you feel about the

event. Be sure not to confuse feelings with thoughts. Rather than saying, "I feel as if my sister thinks I'm stupid" (which is actually a belief), instead, describe how you feel about your sister thinking you're stupid. Are you feeling angry? Do you feel hurt? Are you indignant? Do you feel vulnerable?

Your *Automatic Thoughts* are the beliefs attached to and the meaning you have assigned to events. What did you say to yourself in response to the event? What went through your mind? For example, an automatic thought associated with the event, "shopping with my sister," might be "My sister thinks I have no judgment in clothes." It is important to pinpoint the automatic thought that is causing your feelings of anger, hurt, or vulnerability.

Is THIS Your Chuck?

Beck and his colleagues[55] recommend monitoring your thoughts and identifying how they have become

[55] Beck, A. T., Kovacs, M., & Weissman, A. (1979). Assessment of suicidal intention: The Scale for Suicide Ideation. *Journal of Consulting and Clinical Psychology*, 47(2), 343-352.

distorted so that you can choose the most appropriate response.  For example, see if you recognize any of your Chuck's distorted thoughts here:

- *Mental Filtering*: focusing on the negative details and magnifying them, while filtering out all positive aspects of a situation.  This is a very common "Chuck-like" behavior, particularly a Chuck who is evaluating a person or situation.  Think about a performance situation in which Chuck focuses on all the things you are doing "wrong," rather than those things you are doing "right."

- *Dichotomous Thinking*: Things are either/or, black/white, good/bad, perfect or a complete failure. There is no "gray" area, no middle ground.

- *Mind Reading*: Chuck can suddenly read minds and know exactly what people are thinking, especially with regard to him.  Unfortunately, this generally results in even more distorted and dichotomous thinking.

- *Catastrophic Exaggeration*: Chuck believes the worst-case scenario is going to occur (i.e., think Chicken Little's "the sky is falling) and for him, it will be intolerable and unfixable.

- *Blaming Others*: This is a classic example of holding other people solely responsible for Chuck's situation, particularly if the outcomes are not favorable or positive to him.

- *Externally Controlled*: Chuck feels completely at the mercy of external forces and believes he will never be able to regain control. This often results in paranoia that causes Chuck to suspect others of nefarious behavior.

## Assessing the Validity of Automatic Thoughts

To determine whether a belief is completely accurate ask yourself, "What evidence do I have to support the belief?" and "What evidence do I have that refutes it?" These questions are useful in identifying thoughts that are biased in that they do not consider all available information. Beliefs

like, "I've made a complete fool of myself" and, "No one

likes me" are almost always distorted.

Draw a line down the middle of a piece of paper and

put the data supporting the automatic thought on the left side

and the data that refutes it on the right side. If you have any

data whatsoever on the right side (usually there will be at

least some), then the automatic thought is necessarily biased

or missing data.

Once you have determined the legitimacy or

illegitimacy of your automatic thoughts you will need to

decide how to change your reaction to them. One way to do

this is to decide on *Logical Comebacks* that provide you

another response to the event, rather than allowing the

automatic ones to continue unrestrained. In other words,

what would be a more realistic way of thinking? What

modifications to the belief would make it more balanced?

In the above example, it is apparent that the automatic

thought, "My sister thinks I'm stupid" or "My sister thinks I have no judgment in clothes" was probably distorted at the very least. A much more realistic interpretation might be something like, "The fact that my sister gives me advice on which clothes to buy tells me she cares about my appearance. I generally DO look good in the clothes she's recommended in the past."

It is important to capitalize on every opportunity to counter automatic negative thoughts. In time, if you keep at it, you will notice that a reasonable examination of automatic thoughts will become second nature—maybe even automatic!


## How to Deal with Chuck's Impatience and Anger

Those of you with an impatient or angry "Chuck" take note: his outbursts are usually not specifically <u>caused</u> by you, so don't internalize them. However, they are <u>directed</u> at you, so you still have to deal with them. The key is that *you* must take on the vulnerability of the situation as you hold a conversation with Chuck about his behavior.

In the moment, when you are in the path of Chuck's lack of patience or anger, take a breath, and find a filter phrase that you can say, such as, "That's an interesting point of view" or "I can appreciate that you want to share this with me." This will give your brain a few precious seconds to think about what has been said and how to respond, increasing your "stimulus-response gap." In other words, it allows your reptilian brain to confront the "fight or flight" response it automatically generates with a more rational one.

Later, though, you will need to confront an emotionally _un_intelligent Chuck; otherwise, you will start developing latent anger toward him. Here are some tips:

- Begin by asking to have a one-on-one meeting with Chuck and recount what <u>you</u> heard and how his impatient or angry behavior made <u>you</u> feel.

- Pay attention to Chuck's emotional reaction. BUT...don't fight emotion with emotion. Respond calmly no matter what he says (again, your filter phrase comes in handy here).

- Tell Chuck the impact that his reaction had on you. Describe how it affects your work, your motivation, your performance, etc.

- Help each other figure out what you could do differently going forward.

- Get agreement and thank him for having the discussion with you.

It is important to recognize that you will not change Chuck and may not even change his responses to you. But using some of these approaches will allow you to react differently than you have been doing. And, for what it's worth when dealing with an emotionally immature "Chuck," that alone may provide some comfort and perception of control for you!

In the next chapter, we look at the issue of delegation—one of the most problematic challenges for both Control Freaks <u>and</u> Approval-holics.

# CHAPTER 8

## The Challenge of Delegation

### Challenge #2:  Inability or Unwillingness to Delegate

*Don't tell people how to do things; tell them what to do and let them surprise you with their results.*
                                        –General George S. Patton

Not surprisingly, the relationship between emotions, like impatience and anger, and delegation is often a strong one.  Sometimes we refuse to delegate, because we don't have the patience to wait for someone to learn something new.  And for many leaders, like the retail manager Chuck in our original example in Chapter 1, their unwillingness to delegate is primarily because of the fear associated with giving up control.  Delegation takes emotional courage when we allow others the opportunity to make mistakes on projects for which we are ultimately responsible.  Emotional courage requires patience, belief in others, respect for another's perception of how a task is done, the purpose of a task or

156

project, and in how much importance is placed on the quality

of the outcome. When leaders are unable or unwilling to

delegate, however, they send a powerful message to

employees: *I don't trust you!*

Research on delegation generally indicates that

leaders and managers who delegate authority to those who

are most likely to be affected by the decision or outcome

have higher performing businesses.[56] Of course, if

subordinates feel that the leader is only delegating tasks he or

she doesn't want to do, they are given too little authority to

be effective in the task, or they feel they are being

micromanaged by the leader, delegation does not result in

happier followers or higher performing organizations.[57]

Interestingly, sometimes we shouldn't trust others to

do a task for which the outcome is too important, dangerous,

or visible. In such cases, we are making a conscious decision

to accept personal responsibility for a project, thereby

---

[56] Miller, D. and Toulouse, J.M. (1986). Strategy, Structure, CEO Personality, and Performance in Small Firms. *American Journal of Small Business*, Winter, 47-62.
[57] Bass, B. (1990). *Bass and Stodgill's Handbook of Leadership, 3rd Edition*. New York: Free Press.

making sure we do not set up another person for failure. This is ultimately a leadership decision. If we make the decision not to delegate, we shouldn't feel badly about not doing so. That is, we shouldn't complain about all the work or time involved, and we must accept the credit or blame for the success or the failure of the project or task. But more often than not, a leader hesitates to delegate because he or she believes it is just easier to do it alone and not involve another person. This decision does not reflect leadership courage; rather, it is a need on the part of the leader to control either the outcome or the process or a need to gain approval for our competence. Consider this Chuck's situation in the following scenario:

### Do You Know a "I'll-Do-It-Myself" Chuck?

Chuck is a star in her job. In fact, she's so good that her boss has promoted her to Sales Manager just one year after he hired her as a Sales Representative.

*"I really love my job,"* she said during one of our coaching sessions, *"but I realize I have a lot to learn about leading,"* she confessed. *"My employees are asking me for more responsibility, and yet I hesitate to delegate the grunt work, so I end up doing it all myself...besides, it takes longer to explain it than to do it. My boss is thrilled with my results, and I don't want to do anything to mess that up with him. But, it's wearing me out!"*

As a salesperson, this Chuck has always been a sole performer who has had total control over her own work. The shift to delegating part of her work feels uncomfortable, because she feels accountable for the results, and she wants it done right. Like most new managers, she thinks that asking others to do work assigned to her means that she is acting irresponsibly or that she doesn't have the competence to do it herself. However, her need for control is also limiting her ability to take on more than just routine work; in essence, she isn't able to see that her *employees can help her* by taking on some of the routine work so that she can begin to do more challenging tasks. In addition, she doesn't recognize that *she can help her employees* by allowing them to develop insights into the fundamentals of the daily running of a department.

Perfectionist tendencies on Chuck's part have both approval and control needs underlying them. On the one hand, she doesn't trust others to do the work the way she would do it. In addition, she wants her boss' approval, and she fears doing "anything to mess that up with him." Chuck also appears to need approval from her employees; otherwise, she wouldn't feel badly about giving them "grunt work." She may even fear that her employees will discover an even better or more efficient way of doing the work. And, for someone with approval needs, that could also provide a small threat to her self-esteem.

Notice, too, her need to control the <u>way</u> the work is done, not just the work product. This control need indicates that she has some obsession with process. I'm sure we have all encountered parents, spouses, or teachers that have major rules on how something must be done: a mother's way to fold bath towels, a husband's way to mow the grass, a teacher's requirements for a term paper. Giving employees broad guidelines is fine, but we all become discouraged and annoyed when our leaders micromanage our work. In fact, we often wonder why the boss just doesn't do it herself!

The challenge this Chuck finds more daunting will depend upon whether control or approval is the more dominant need, i.e., the need to control the work and how it is done, or the need for approval from her boss and her employees. But this can shift as the situation and context changes. As one person's leadership development plan noted,

> *My case is an example of two extremes. On one side is my need to control everything. I want things done my way, to my standards. If people get in the way, then they get run over. On the other side is my need for approval. This comes from being the middle of six children. My goal was to keep everyone happy, and I've carried that with me into the business world. My behavior continually shifts between the two extremes of control and approval.*

## How to Deal with Chuck's Unwillingness to Delegate

For a new leader like architect Chuck in our initial example, delegation poses a particular struggle between the need for approval from his boss and the need for approval from his blue-collar subordinates. On the one hand, delegation recognizes that subordinates will inevitably make mistakes, but that the learning that takes place will ultimately result in higher quality work. If Chuck is primarily concerned with garnering approval from his exemplary subordinates, he will be more likely to delegate. On the other hand, delegation also requires trust in one's own ability to be accountable for the outcomes. If Chuck is most concerned with approval from his boss, he may not be comfortable with shouldering the responsibility for his subordinates' mistakes and, therefore, would be less likely to delegate.

If your Chuck has a high need for control, his failure to delegate likely stems from perfectionism (he doesn't trust you to do it "his" way or achieve the outcome "he" wants). To encourage Chuck to delegate, try appealing to his challenge of being overwhelmed by saying something like this:

> *I sense that you are feeling overwhelmed by this project, and I'd like to take some small part of it off your plate. I want to make sure I meet your expectations, of course, so I will report on my progress daily (or weekly, or monthly). What task might I do that you feel would help you most?*

If your Chuck has high approval needs, focus on the kudos he will get from his boss when the project is done correctly and on time:

> *I know how important it is to you to get this project done right and by next Wednesday. Think how pleased Ms. Boss will be when we are able to deliver it by her deadline, maybe even earlier! Divvying up the work and giving you time to check it all ahead of time makes us all look good.*

Delegation is ultimately a trust issue, whether Chuck is a Control Freak or an Approval-holic. Realize that your Chuck will have to be brought along slowly. Taking baby steps to show him or her that you will deliver on your promises will result in increased delegation over time.

## Working on Your Own Delegation Challenges

You may have your own challenges with delegation, too. Clearly, the first step is to figure out whether your reluctance to delegate is being driven primarily by a need to control or by a need to receive approval (or avoid disapproval). If control is your primary driving force, try these actions to improve your delegation abilities:

- ***Take stock of your "To Do" list***, and check the tasks that are routine or require few instructions or elaborate guidelines. Despite the fact that you will need to explain some of the WHAT, WHY, and WHEN, consider that this is a long-term investment, because the next time there will be less need for explanations.

- ***Spell out the results needed, and set up interim meetings to check progress, coach, or advise.***

Otherwise, HANDS OFF! Rather than evaluate how the task is done, ask yourself, "Do these results accomplish what is needed?"

- ***Clearly indicate how much authority employees will have in the given task, so they don't have to ask you for your approval at each step.*** If you let your employees have some decision-making authority, they will take more responsibility for their work because the end result will be their own.

- ***Do not delegate assignments that require a lot of judgment, complex decision-making, or that a senior manager has asked you to personally handle.*** Do not delegate work that has high visibility or is accompanied by a high level of risk. In other words, don't set up employees for failure. Only delegate those tasks for which employees are well-prepared or for which their visibility would be beneficial to them or to you.

- ***Don't delegate all the junk and keep the good stuff for yourself***, or your employees will become bored and, what's worse, they will feel that you don't trust them to do the "important" work. And if your employees can't do at least some of the "important" work, you are to blame. Expose employees to more and more complex assignments so they learn to handle them.

If approval is your primary driving force, try these actions to improve your delegation abilities:

- ***Do not delegate with an apologetic tone.*** Employees aren't doing you a favor; you are giving them a chance to find challenge in their work and growth in their careers.
- ***Always communicate the same information to one employee as to another.*** Don't have different stories for different employees. You want your employees to believe you trust them, so if you

want them to be able to do the work you are delegating, they must not feel as if they aren't being told what others are being told.

- And although you are ultimately responsible for the work you delegate, ***don't blame employees if things go wrong.*** Meet with employees to find out what happened and why and to look for ways to avoid making the same mistakes again. Send a powerful message that you do not consider employees' failures when they make a mistake. Employees appreciate and respond positively when you are able to separate the person from his or her behavior.

Ultimately, delegation requires you to face a trust and trustworthiness issue, both in yourself and in your employees. Your ability to understand what drives your fear about delegating will help you to focus your development efforts.

Of course, part of poor delegation often has to do with not explaining things well enough so that expectations about process or outcomes are clear.  In the next chapter, we look into the very common challenge of communication— and it isn't necessarily caused by what you think it is!

# CHAPTER 9

## The Challenge of Communication

*Bad human communication leaves us less room to grow.*
—Rowan Williams, Archbishop of Canterbury (2002-2012)

### *Challenge #3 - Communicating with Others*

So much has been written, discussed, and blamed on communication failures that I hesitate even dealing with this topic. It always seems so obvious, doesn't it? Just communicate *better!* However, this is much easier said than done for most of us, primarily because we are not always sure what *better* really means. Should I communicate more? Should I communicate less? Should I speak face-to-face, over the phone, or in writing? Which is most appropriate? Which is *better*?

Of course, there is no one *better* means of communication. It depends on the person, the situation, the issue, and the value to the receiver. Daft and Lengel[58] and many other researchers have done excellent work in the area of "media richness," advocating that the more important the message, the more personal and "rich"[59] the means should be of conveying it. For example, if you must terminate one of your subordinates, you certainly shouldn't leave a voice mail message, but sit down face-to-face with him or her.

But the medium and its richness are merely the *mechanics* of communication. From the deep-seated roots of approval and control, we might shed some light on what is really at the heart of these problems, and it generally has little to do with mechanics.

---

[58] See, for example, Daft, R.L. & Lengel, R.H. (1984). Information richness: a new approach to managerial behavior and organizational design. In: Cummings, L.L. & Staw, B.M. (Eds.), *Research in organizational behavior 6, (191-233)*. Homewood, IL: JAI Press; Daft, R.L., Lengel, R.H., & Trevino, L.K. (1987). Message equivocality, media selection, and manager performance: Implications for information systems. *MIS Quarterly*, 355-366.

[59] *Richness* refers to the use of multiple modes of communication, such as words, facial expressions, voice inflection, gestures, touch, symbols, writing, etc. to convey more meaning and subtext information.

## The Communication Problem with Chuck

Many of us have a Chuck that has difficulty communicating. There are myriad ways that we get frustrated with the "how" and "when" Chuck shares or requests information. However, the problem that generally drives you the craziest probably falls into one of two categories: withholding information or manipulating information. In other words, Chuck doesn't tell you what you need to know when you need to know it, or Chuck changes his story depending upon who he's talking to.

In the first case, Chuck may believe that "knowledge is power." In other words, if he tells you what he knows, you will have as much power as he does. "Chucks" often believe that one way to show their power is to have more information than everybody else, and that means they tend to keep secret much of the information that should be shared. This clearly is derived from their high need to control people, information, and situations.

But how does that actually work to give them more power? In other words, how does Chuck actually demonstrate that he has power?

*Chuck has to tell the secret to someone!* That way, other people think, "Wow...Chuck is in the know." Coincidentally, that is why there are rarely many secrets in organizations. Of course, the ironic outcome of telling a secret is that he actually <u>loses</u> trust and credibility with others and, ultimately, his power.

Dealing with a less-than-forthcoming Chuck requires that we cultivate other sources of information and ask good questions. As we hear rumors or gossip about things that directly affect us, it is a good idea to validate them with multiple people. Common sense tells us that relying on only one source may not provide accurate or truthful information anyway.

It is also likely that our Chuck may like to pretend he knows things, but he really doesn't. By providing accurate information yourself on those issues that have consequences for our departments or our work, we create our own credibility and trustworthiness.

Chuck's second communication problem—his tendency to manipulate people and information—stems from high needs for both control and approval. Imagine you work in Accounts Receivable and are talking with your Chuck about an issue with a major customer's overdue payment. You describe the problem to Chuck, and he says, "I'll call them today and make sure they pay in the next week." You end the conversation, thinking that the problem will be solved. Later, Chuck talks with the customer and tells them, "Just get your payment in as soon as you can." Another month goes by, and no payment is forthcoming. You talk to Chuck again, and he tells you that he made it very clear the payment was due by the end of the month.

Now what?

He's put you in an awkward position, hasn't he? He told you one thing and the customer another. It is likely that Chuck wants to be seen as solidly in control of the situation, and he wants your approval as a capable co-worker. He also seeks approval from the major customer (so the customer doesn't get mad and Chuck is blamed for losing the account). It is also likely that Chuck tends to avoid conflict, so having an honest discussion about payment with a major customer is likely a huge challenge for him.

The only real way to deal with a Chuck in this type of situation is to document your encounters and ask direct and specific questions. If Chuck is a peer or your boss, this will feel awkward and could rile him. Your own emotional intelligence will alert you to whether or not -this is professionally risky! A less politically-risky strategy is to offer to take the burden of contacting the customer "off his plate," because you know that he is "so busy with other important tasks." Remember—high need for approval folks see such statements as validating their worth. And, if your Chuck is has a high need for control, it allows him to delegate the task without appearing weak or incompetent.

It's All About the Relationship

Covey's statement, "The key to better communication is a healthy one-on-one relationship,"[60] is an intriguing one. His point is that it is difficult to communicate with those who are distant and in whom you have little trust. But the Catch-22 here is that in order to develop a healthy, trusting relationship with someone, you must have trustworthy communication.

But what does that really mean?

Basically, at its core, it is *truthfulness, vulnerability, and authenticity*. Every time we act and speak from truth, we invite those we communicate with to do the same. Each time that we distort the truth, we constrict and limit the depth of what we are and what our relationship with that person can become. We limit beliefs about ourselves and what we are capable of becoming. For many of us, open communication presents a fear that the truth will unleash a torrent of anger or rejection. But, merely colluding with each other to stay in

---

[60] Covey, S.R. (1990). *Principle-Centered Leadership.* New York: Fireside.

safe territory and avoid difficult issues means that we are settling for much less than what we might experience with another person. We have to invite vulnerability from ourselves and those with whom we communicate.

As Brené Brown writes, "Vulnerability sounds like truth and feels like courage. Truth and courage aren't always comfortable, but they're never weakness."[61] The problem with vulnerability is that it feels like courage in ourselves, but it looks like weakness in others. For those of us with deeply rooted control and approval needs, showing that we are vulnerable seems to risk a loss of control or disapproval from others. But most at risk is our own credibility and trustworthiness.

## What Effective Communicators Do

Research has shown that being an effective communicator is based on five interpersonal components:

---

[61] Brown, B. (2012). *Daring greatly: How the courage to be vulnerable transforms the way we live, love, parent, and lead*. New York, NY: Gotham Books.

1. An adequate self-concept, the single most important factor affecting people's communication with others;

2. The ability to be a good listener, a skill which often has received little attention;

3. The skill of expressing one's thoughts and ideas clearly, which many people find difficult to do;

4. Being able to cope with one's emotions, particularly angry feelings, and expressing them in a constructive way; and

5. The willingness to disclose oneself to others truthfully and freely. Such self-disclosure is necessary for satisfactory interpersonal relationships, but it requires vulnerability.[62]

As these components suggest, much of the success we achieve in communicating with others is based partly on skill and mechanics (e.g., listening, expressing thoughts clearly,

---

[62] M.J. Bienvenu, Sr. (1971). An interpersonal communication inventory. *The Journal of Communication*, 21, pp. 381-388.

and emotional control) and partly on our ability to be authentic, vulnerable, truthful, and forthcoming. Commitment to the truth can be uncomfortable and scary at times, but it is also the surest path to ongoing emotional growth and deepening interpersonal connections.

If you have struggled with this before, it's time to be honest about it and to take steps to understand why you might have been less than honest in the past. Ask yourself, "what healing needs to take place within me so that I no longer need to hide or appear different than who I really am?" In other words, your understanding of your high need for control and/or approval is paramount for understanding why you may have trouble communicating with (and, thus, relating to) a coworker, boss, or direct report. And remember, the commitment to the truth is not necessarily sharing something negative. The truth can be about the positive aspects of your relationship, organization, projects, employees, and life.

## Fear of Public Presentations

In addition to the general problem with honest and authentic interpersonal communication, many people struggle with the fear of standing in front of a group of people and speaking. We may all have a bit of this fear of public speaking; in fact, it is one of the most feared activities for most people. Like Jerry Seinfeld once said, "At a funeral, most people would rather in be in the casket than giving the eulogy."

But most of this fear is "**F**alse **E**xpectations **A**ppearing **R**eal." In essence, there are underlying causes for why many of us avoid public speaking, and most of them are figments of our imaginations. For example, Morton C. Orman, M.D., FLP lists the following underlying causes for the stress caused by this fear, but he goes on to say that most of these are not accurate reflections of reality:

- Thinking that public speaking is inherently stressful;
- Thinking you need to be brilliant or perfect to succeed;

- Trying to impart too much information or cover too many points in a short presentation;

- Having the wrong purpose in mind (to get, rather than to give/contribute);

- Trying to please everyone;

- Trying to emulate other speakers, rather than simply being yourself;

- Failing to be personally revealing and humble;

- Being fearful of potential negative outcomes;

- Trying to control the wrong things (e.g., the behavior of your audience);

- Spending too much time preparing, instead of developing confidence and trust in your natural ability to succeed;

- Thinking your audience will be as critical of your performance as you might be.[63]

---

[63] Orman, M.C., MD, FLP,
https://sajidocean.wordpress.com/category/how-to-conquer-public-speaking-fear-by-morton-c-orman/ Retrieved October 24, 2016.

As we saw in dealing with automatic thoughts, these distortions of reality are created by us in response to events and our feelings surrounding them. Although we may never have had any of these experiences, we fear them because we can't control them. And, for many of us whose approval needs drive our fears, we fear rejection and shame from those who might hear us speak. It's a real fear for many people, but the only way to deal with this one is to do it. That's right...practicing is the <u>only</u> way to overcome one's fear of public speaking!

## Working on Your Own Public Speaking

Many people have found Toastmaster's International to be a very helpful group. Their practice meetings each week or each month provide members with a host of opportunities to give public speeches and presentations to others who are interested in improving their public speaking abilities, too. They create a safe environment, and most people report tremendous improvement in a fairly short period of time.  To find a Toastmaster's meeting near you, visit their website at http://www.toastmasters.org/find/.  It will be a worthwhile investment in your development.

Finding ways to communicate more truthfully, as well as volunteering to practice speaking in a public forum, are vitally important development activities for all of us.  I encourage you to include "improved communication" targets in your development plans, no matter how well you believe you communicate now.  You might also enjoy taking the *Interpersonal Communication Inventory*[64] at the end of this chapter to see what aspects of communication you need to work on, whether it is interpersonal conflict, conveying your feelings, or explaining complex ideas.

All of us can get better at conveying our thoughts and feelings to others, encouraging and affirming them, and clarifying our expectations, needs, and goals.  It just takes practice.

---

[64] Bienvenu, M.J. (1971). An interpersonal communication inventory. *The Journal of Communication*, 21, 381-388.

As a unique case of interpersonal communication, handling conflict is a particularly difficult challenge for many of us. Whether you are a Control Freak or an Approval-holic, conflict with friends, family, peers, bosses, or direct reports is uncomfortable. In the next chapter, we'll spend a bit of time understanding types of conflict and the challenges they provide to those of us with high control and approval needs.

# Interpersonal Communication Inventory[65]

*Directions*
- Answer each question as quickly as you can according to the way you usually feel.
- Do not consult anyone while completing the inventory.
- Honest answers are very necessary. Please be as frank as possible.
- Read each question carefully. If you cannot give the exact answer to a question, answer the best you can, but be sure to answer each one. There is no right or wrong answer.

|  | Yes (usually) | Sometimes | No (rarely) |
|---|---|---|---|
| 1. Do your words come out the way you would like them to in conversation? | | | |
| 2. When you are asked a question that is not clear, do you ask the person to explain what he means? | | | |
| 3. When you are trying to explain something, do other persons have a tendency to put words in your mouth? | | | |
| 4. Do you merely assume the other person knows what you are trying to say without your explaining what you really mean? | | | |
| 5. Do you ever ask the other person to tell you how he feels about the point you may be trying to make? | | | |
| 6. Is it difficult for you to talk with other people? | | | |
| 7. In conversation, do you talk about things which are of interest to both you and the other person? | | | |
| 8. Do you find it difficult to express your ideas when they differ from those around you? | | | |
| 9. In conversation, do you try to put yourself in the other person's shoes? | | | |

[65] Bienvenu, M.J. (1971). An interpersonal communication inventory. *The Journal of Communication*, 21, 381-388.

| | Yes (usually) | Sometimes | No (rarely) |
|---|---|---|---|
| 10. In conversation, do you have a tendency to do more talking than the other person? | | | |
| 11. Are you aware of how your tone of voice may affect others? | | | |
| 12. Do you refrain from saying something that you know will hurt others or make matters worse? | | | |
| 13. Is it difficult to accept constructive criticism from others? | | | |
| 14. When someone has hurt your feelings, do you discuss this with them? | | | |
| 15. Do you later apologize to someone whose feelings you may have hurt? | | | |
| 16. Does it upset you a great deal when someone disagrees with you? | | | |
| 17. Do you find it difficult to think clearly when you are angry with someone? | | | |
| 18. Do you fail to disagree with others because you are afraid they will get angry? | | | |
| 19. When a problem arises between you and another person can you discuss it without getting angry? | | | |
| 20. Are you satisfied with the way you settle your differences with others? | | | |
| 21. Do you pout and sulk for a long time when someone upsets you? | | | |
| 22. Do you become very uneasy when someone pays you a compliment? | | | |
| 23. Generally, are you able to trust other individuals? | | | |
| 24. Do you find it difficult to compliment/praise others? | | | |
| 25. Do you deliberately try to conceal your faults? | | | |

| | Yes (usually) | Sometimes | No (rarely) |
|---|---|---|---|
| 26. Do you help others to understand you by saying how you think, feel, and believe? | | | |
| 27. Is it difficult for you to confide in people? | | | |
| 28. Do you have a tendency to change the subject when your feelings enter into a discussion? | | | |
| 29. In conversation, do you let the other person finish talking before reacting to what he says? | | | |
| 30. Do you find yourself not paying attention while in conversation with others? | | | |
| 31. Do you ever try to listen for meaning when someone is talking? | | | |
| 32. Do others seem to be listening when you're talking? | | | |
| 33. In a discussion, is it difficult for you to see things from the other person's point of view? | | | |
| 34. Do you pretend you are listening to others when actually you are not? | | | |
| 35. In conversation, can you tell the difference between what a person is saying and what he may be feeling? | | | |
| 36. While speaking, are you aware of how others are reacting to what you are saying? | | | |
| 37. Do you feel that other people wish you were a different kind of person? | | | |
| 38. Do you believe that other people understand your feelings? | | | |
| 39. Do others remark that you always seem to think you are right? | | | |
| 40. Do you admit that you are wrong when you know that you are wrong about something? | | | |

**Scoring Key and Norms:** Look at how you responded to each item. In front of the item, mark the appropriate weight from the table. For example, if you answered "Yes" to item 1, you would find below that you get three points. Then add up your total score and compare your score to the norms listed on the following page.

| | Yes | No | Sometimes | Your Score |
|---|---|---|---|---|
| 1. | 3 | 0 | 2 | |
| 2. | 3 | 0 | 2 | |
| 3. | 0 | 3 | 1 | |
| 4. | 0 | 3 | 1 | |
| 5. | 3 | 0 | 2 | |
| 6. | 0 | 3 | 1 | |
| 7. | 3 | 0 | 2 | |
| 8. | 0 | 3 | 1 | |
| 9. | 3 | 0 | 2 | |
| 10. | 0 | 3 | 1 | |
| 11. | 3 | 0 | 2 | |
| 12. | 3 | 0 | 2 | |
| 13. | 0 | 3 | 1 | |
| 14. | 3 | 0 | 2 | |
| 15. | 3 | 0 | 2 | |
| 16. | 0 | 3 | 1 | |
| 17. | 0 | 3 | 1 | |
| 18. | 0 | 3 | 1 | |
| 19. | 3 | 0 | 2 | |
| 20. | 3 | 0 | 2 | |
| 21. | 0 | 3 | 1 | |
| 22. | 0 | 3 | 1 | |
| 23. | 3 | 0 | 2 | |
| 24. | 0 | 3 | 1 | |
| 25. | 0 | 3 | 1 | |
| 26. | 3 | 0 | 2 | |
| 27. | 0 | 3 | 1 | |
| 28. | 0 | 3 | 1 | |
| 29. | 3 | 0 | 2 | |
| 30. | 0 | 3 | 1 | |
| 31. | 3 | 0 | 2 | |
| 32. | 3 | 0 | 2 | |
| 33. | 0 | 3 | 1 | |
| 34. | 0 | 3 | 1 | |
| 35. | 3 | 0 | 2 | |
| 36. | 3 | 0 | 2 | |
| 37. | 0 | 3 | 1 | |

| | | | | |
|------|---|---|---|---|
| 38. | 3 | 0 | 2 | |
| 39. | 0 | 3 | 1 | |
| 40. | 3 | 0 | 2 | |
| **Your Total** | | | | |

*Compare your score to the means of those for your age and gender.*

## Means and Standard Deviations for the ICI

| Age Groups | Males | Females |
|---|---|---|
| 22-25 | Mean....81.70<br>SD............21.56 | Mean.....81.48<br>SD.............20.06 |
| 26 and up | Mean....90.73<br>SD............14.74 | Mean....94.46<br>SD.............11.58 |
| All age groups | Mean....86.39<br>SD............19.46 | Mean.... 85.34<br>SD.............18.22 |

# CHAPTER 10

## The Challenge of Conflict

*Do not think of knocking out another person's brains because he differs in opinion from you. It would be as rational to knock yourself on the head because you differ from yourself ten years ago.*
      — Horace Mann, 1st Massachusetts Sec. of Education
        (1796 – 1859)

### *Challenge #4:  Avoiding or Mishandling Conflict Situations*

Conflict is basically a disagreement through which everybody involved perceives a threat to their needs, interests, values, or goals.  Inevitably, we will have disagreements and conflicts with those with whom we work, lead, and follow.  Whether they are brought out in the open or left unsaid, disagreements are a part of life.  Reasonable people often disagree, and that is to be expected and, in some cases, welcomed.  Conflict is a necessary part of truth seeking.  When we avoid dealing with conflict, it festers and becomes disruptive.  Generally, conflict is most destructive when it stems from emotional responses to our disagreements.

As members of an organization, we are called to community, not unity, of opinion. We become effective when we learn how to manage conflict, not avoid it. We certainly don't want to be like the couple that explained to the marriage counselor, "We never talk any more. We figured out that's when we have all our fights."

Unfortunately, like the married couple, many of us avoid conflict like the plague, mainly because of a need to avoid disapproval from others, as evidenced in this leadership plan excerpt:

> *The reason that I avoid conflict is that I am a people-pleaser. I don't want to hurt peoples' feelings, and I want people to like me. If I argue or confront people with a controversial issue, their approval of my decision and me, personally, may be jeopardized. The problem that results from my avoidance of conflict is that I fail to get my point across and get the problem truly solved. If I work to make someone happy just to stop the confrontation, then I am not*

*doing my job effectively—issues are not being*
*properly addressed, and problems will never be*
*solved.*

## What is Your Conflict with Chuck About?

If you are like most people, most of the conflicts with your Chuck center on at least one of the following areas:

- **Goal Conflict**. You and Chuck have conflicting goals or priorities, e.g., you want to focus on a new strategic opportunity; Chuck wants to focus on a current operational problem.

- **Personalit**y **Conflict**. A common problem, you and Chuck haven't figured out an effective way to relate to each other. A personality conflict usually has to do with differences in behavior or upbringing. For example, if you are a naturally positive and optimistic person, you may have difficulty dealing with someone who has a negative attitude.

- **Resource Conflict**. Conflict can happen when you're competing over scarce resources. If you and Chuck are peers, and one of you seems to be getting more resources from your boss (e.g., staff, money, time) than is the other, that can cause conflict between you, and perhaps between you and your boss, too.

- **Information Processing Conflict**. People have different work processing styles. Your thinking style or communication style might conflict with Chuck's thinking style or his communication style. For example, there are some of us who focus on the "big picture" and some of us who focus on the details of a project. Another example is that some of us "talk as we think," while some of us "think before we talk." All of these can cause conflict in our relationships with others who process information differently.

- **Values Conflict**. Values are core, both to individuals and to organizations. It is why many people find that a particular boss, co-worker, organization, or culture just clashes with them. For example, Chuck may value how much work you accomplish; you may value the quality of what you accomplish more than how much work you actually did. Values conflicts are some of the most difficult to resolve, primarily because values are so deeply entrenched in people and in companies.

Whichever conflict tends to plague you and Chuck, engaging in dialogue and negotiation around conflict is something most of us tend to approach with fear and hesitation, afraid that the conversation will make the conflict worse. All too often, we talk ourselves out of having a dialogue, because it takes courage to honestly and clearly articulate your needs and to sit down and listen to those in disagreement with you. It takes courage to look at your own role in the dispute, and it takes courage to approach others with a sense of empathy, openness, and respect for their perspective.

## How Do You Deal with Conflict?

Most experts agree that addressing conflict in the workplace centers on the mix of how important the relationship is and how important the outcome is to the parties in conflict. Theories of cooperation and competition recognize that people have different motives for reaching agreement. Some people are concerned about outcomes, i.e., getting what they want (known as "claiming value") and the relationship with the other person, as well as making sure that the other person gets what she wants, too (known as "creating value"). As a result, they exchange information to build trust and uncover tradeoffs for mutual benefit. This approach is considered a *prosocial* approach to conflict resolution.

Other people are concerned more with their own outcomes, with little concern for the other party achieving desired outcomes or whether there can be an ongoing relationship with the other party.[66] In essence, the

---

importance for them is claiming value or "slicing the pie" for their own benefit. This approach is considered an *egoistic* approach to conflict resolution.

Overall, we call these two concerns the "the dual concerns model" of conflict resolution, and there are five primary styles or approaches that are used when confronted with a conflict or dispute.[67] The following model in Figure 1 shows the relationship between concerns for the relationship ("Cooperative") and concerns for getting desired outcomes ("Assertive"):

**Figure 1. The Dual Concerns Model of Conflict Resolution**

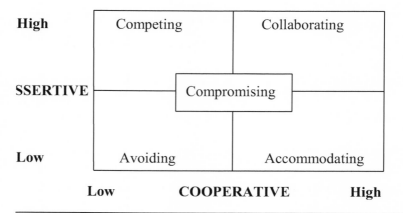

[66] Deutsch, M. (1973). *The resolution of conflict: Constructive and destructive processes.* New Haven, Conn: Yale University Press.
[67] Thomas, K. W. and Kilmann, R. H. (1974). *Thomas-Kilmann Conflict Mode Instrument.* Mountain Vcxiew, CA: Xicom, a subsidiary of CPP, Inc.

Creating value is a collaborative venture with a counterpart that requires creativity and problem-solving ability. Whereas, claiming value is more competitive.

However, part of the ability and willingness to create and claim value may have to do with an overall need for assertiveness and cooperation. Underlying needs for control and approval may help predict the extent to which an individual is assertive in claiming value (higher in control) or cooperative in creating value (higher in approval).

## The Role of Control and Approval

*Collaborating* results from a high concern for your own interests, matched with a high concern for the interests of another. The outcome is "win/win." This strategy is generally used when concerns for others are important. This approach helps build commitment and reduce bad feelings. The drawbacks are that it takes time and energy. In addition, some people may take advantage of the other's trust and openness. Generally regarded as the best approach for managing conflict, the objective of collaboration is to reach consensus. Persons who have a healthy balance between needs for control and approval are most likely to adopt this approach.

*Compromising* results from a high concern for your own interests, along with a moderate concern for the interests of another. The outcome is "win some/lose some." This strategy is generally used to achieve temporary solutions, to avoid destructive power struggles, or when time pressures exist. One drawback is that partners can lose sight of important values and long-term objectives. This approach can also distract the partners from the merits of an issue and create a cynical climate. Persons who usually adopt a compromise strategy have low to moderate needs for both control and approval.

*Competing* results from a high concern for your own interests and less concern for others. The outcome is "win/lose." This strategy is generally used when basic rights are at stake or to set a precedent. However, it can cause the conflict to escalate and the "losers" may try to retaliate. By far, persons who act competitively to deal with conflict are high in their need for control and low in their need for approval.

*Accommodating* results from a low concern for your own interests, combined with a high concern for the interests of another. The outcome is "lose/win." This strategy is generally used when the issue is more important to others than to you. It is a "goodwill gesture." It is also appropriately used when you recognize that you are wrong. The drawbacks are that your own ideas and concerns don't get attention. You may also lose credibility and future influence. Most persons who rely on accommodation strategies have high approval needs and lower control needs.

*Avoiding* results from a low concern for your own interests, coupled with a low concern for the interests of others. The outcome is "lose/lose." This strategy is generally used when the issue is trivial or other issues are more pressing. It is also used when confrontation has a high potential for damage or when more information is needed. The drawback is that important decisions may be made by default. Avoidance is most often the strategy adopted by those with low control and higher approval needs, although the previous concern about "damage control" makes this a sound initial strategy for all of us whenever the relationship is at stake.

Most of us have a tendency to react to another's behavior with consistency. Your style of dealing with conflicts is probably fairly predictable, although it is certainly true that people's responses to situational conflicts can change. To get a sense of your preferred approach, consider what you might do in this scenario with Chuck:

---

**What is YOUR Approach to Conflict?**

*You are a manager who feels overloaded with projects and paperwork. You work hard to keep things balanced, trying to provide your employees with information and adequate lead time. But, because you are often tied up in meetings or otherwise unavailable, you frequently depend on others to provide information or reports.*

*You recently were asked to work with Chuck, one of your peer managers, on an assignment, the report and presentation for which is due today. Each of you has done some of the report, and Chuck had agreed to finish it up yesterday while you were out of town. But when you arrived at the office this morning, you did not find the finalized report he promised to leave for you on your desk. You call Chuck and ask where he put the report. He said that he did not have time to finish it, as he had to leave the office at 2:00 p.m. yesterday for a dental appointment.*

*Which of these behavioral responses most resembles the one you would have?*

a.   You attend the meeting and present what you can. You approach your boss and blame the incomplete presentation and report on Chuck.

b.   You cancel all the rest of your meetings and appointments and spend the next four hours completing the report yourself. At the presentation, you barely acknowledge that Chuck worked with you on the project.

c.   You say, "OK," hang up, and then shut yourself in your office all morning. Right before the presentation, you have your secretary call to let your boss know that the report will be filed by the end of the day, but you are unable to attend the presentation meeting.

d.   You ask Chuck what suggestions he has for making sure this is done by the presentation meeting. You offer to meet with him to finish this up, and ask him to commit to giving it top priority this morning, so it is completed by the deadline. You repeat the agreement you have both reached and ask him if this is his understanding of what you have agreed to.

Most likely the conflict you are experiencing with Chuck has to do with both *values* and *goals*. Perhaps your goal was to finish the report and present it on time, and your value is keeping the commitments you make, no matter what. His goals and values clearly were different from yours, at least with regard to this task.

The first behavioral choice indicates competition. When you get angry and blame others, you are really engaging in a competitive approach. Chuck, in this case, will probably hear about what you have done, and he will probably lose all respect and trust in you. Many people reading this will probably proclaim, "But...he *is* untrustworthy! I am merely making sure my boss realizes it!" If you think your boss will appreciate you pointing out the flaws in another person, you are sadly mistaken. It is a very adolescent way of dealing with the heart of the matter, which is getting the report and presentation accomplished. How it gets done is most likely not of concern to your boss. Moreover, it ignores the major problem of actually completing the project—an ironic twist, since *you* have not completed it either!

The next two behavioral choices are based on your desire to get the job done. While the fact that you take your responsibility seriously is laudable, it creates tension between you and Chuck that will likely spill over into other interactions that you may have in the future.

In the second choice, your perception that he didn't do much of anything is an over-reaction. The reality is that he didn't do what you wanted or expected him to do it; in this choice, your response is very self-centered. Remember that making someone else look bad does nothing for your own professionalism. Equally inappropriate is withdrawing from the consequences of your action, as the third behavioral choice implies. Using your secretary as the communicator is nothing short of cowardly and triangulates the relationship between you, your secretary, and your boss. It ultimately may leave you feeling ashamed. Avoiding your responsibility only sends a message to your boss that you are untrustworthy.

The last behavioral choice sends a strong leadership message: both you and Chuck are accountable for delivering the report and presentation. While you are sensitive to the fact that he had another commitment, you are not letting him off the hook by ignoring the commitment you both made that the report and presentation would be done today. You are respectful, but remind him that both of you are accountable for finishing what you started. You make sure that he recommits, and you make sure that an understanding is achieved before hanging up.

The bottom line is that collaborative approaches to conflict management require us to engage in dialogue in profound and meaningful ways. Of course, that requires empathy and emotional intelligence, as well as good

communication skills.

## What to Do If You Rely on One Conflict Mode Too Much or Too Little

Thomas and Kilmann[68] suggest that there are various

questions to ask yourself if you are concerned that you may

be competing, collaborating, accommodating, compromising,

or avoiding conflict too frequently or too infrequently:

- If you feel as though you **COMPETE too frequently**, you may wish to ask yourself:
  - Are you surrounded by "yes" people? If so, perhaps it's because they have learned that it's unwise to disagree with you or have given up trying to influence you. This closes you off to information.
  - Are others afraid to admit ignorance and uncertainties to you? In a competitive climate, one must fight for influence and respect, acting more certain and confident than one feels. This means that people are less able to ask for information and opinions – they are less likely to learn.

[68] Thomas, K.W. and Kilmann, R.H. (2007). The Thomas-Kilmann Conflict Mode Instrument. Mountain View, CA: CPP, Inc., 12-16.

- If you feel as though you **COMPETE too infrequently**, you may wish to ask yourself:
  - Do you often feel powerless in situations? You may be unaware of the power you have, unskilled in its use, or uncomfortable with the idea of using it. This may hinder your effectiveness by restricting your influence.
  - Do you sometimes have trouble taking a firm stand, even when you see the need? Sometimes concerns for others' feelings or anxieties about the use of power cause people to vacillate.
- If you feel as though you **ACCOMMODATE too frequently**, you may wish to ask yourself:
  - Do you feel that your ideas and concerns sometimes don't get the attention they deserve? Deferring too much to the concerns of others can deprive you of influence, respect, and recognition. It can also deprive the organization of your potential contributions.
  - Is discipline lax? Although discipline for its own sake may be of little value, some rules and procedures are crucial and need to be enforced. Accommodating on these issues may harm you, others, or the organization.
- If you feel as though you **ACCOMMODATE too infrequently**, you may wish to ask yourself:
  - Do you sometimes have trouble building goodwill with others? Accommodation on minor issues that are important to others is a gesture of goodwill.
  - Do others sometimes seem to regard you as unreasonable?
  - Do you occasionally have trouble admitting when you are wrong?
  - Do you recognize legitimate exceptions to the rules?

- If you feel as though you **COLLABORATE too frequently**, you may wish to ask yourself:
    - Do you sometimes spend time discussing issues in depth that don't seem to warrant it? Collaboration takes time and energy – perhaps the scarcest organizational resources. Trivial problems don't require optimal solution, and not all personal differences need to be hashed out.
    - Does your collaborative behavior fail to elicit collaborative responses from others? The exploratory and tentative nature of some collaborative behavior may make it easy for others to disregard your overtures or take advantage of the trust and openness you display.
- If you feel as though you **COLLABORATE too infrequently**, you may wish to ask yourself:
    - Is it difficult for you to see differences as opportunities for joint gain, learning, or problem-solving? Although conflict situations often involve threatening or unproductive aspects, approaching all conflicts with pessimism can prevent you from seeing collaborative possibilities and thus deprive you of the mutual gains and satisfactions that accompany successful collaboration.
    - Are others uncommitted to your decisions or policies? Perhaps their concerns are not being incorporated into those decisions or policies.
- If you feel as though you **COMPROMISE too frequently**, you may wish to ask yourself:
    - Do you concentrate so heavily on the practicalities and tactics of compromise that you sometimes lose sight of larger issues? Doing so may lead to unintended and costly compromises of principles, values, long-term objectives, or company welfare.
    - Does an emphasis on bargaining and trading create a climate of gamesmanship? Such a

climate may undermine interpersonal trust and deflect attention from the merits of the issues being discussed.

- If you feel as though you **COMPROMISE too infrequently**, you may wish to ask yourself:
    - Do you sometimes find yourself too sensitive or embarrassed to engage in the give-and-take of bargaining?  This reticence can keep you from getting a fair share in negotiations – for yourself, your team, or your organization.
    - Do you sometimes find it difficult to make concessions?  Without this safety valve, you may have trouble gracefully getting out of mutually destructive arguments, power struggles, and so on.
- If you feel as though you **AVOID too frequently**, you may wish to ask yourself:
    - Does coordination suffer because people sometimes have trouble getting your input on issues?
    - Does it sometimes appear that people are "walking on eggshells"?  Sometimes a dysfunctional amount of energy is devoted to caution and avoiding issues, indicating that those issues need to be faced and resolved
    - Are decisions on important issues sometimes made by default?
- If you feel as though you **AVOID too infrequently**, you may wish to ask yourself:
    - Do you sometimes find yourself hurting people's feelings or stirring up hostilities?  You may need to exercise more discretion and tact, framing issues in nonthreatening ways.
    - Do you sometimes feel harried or overwhelmed by a number of issues?  You may need to devote more time to setting priorities – that is, deciding which issues are relatively unimportant and perhaps delegating them to others.

## Working on Managing Conflict with Chuck

Being in conflict doesn't necessarily mean being mad at each other. It *can* mean an opportunity to show your wisdom, to create a better situation, and to help both of you be winners. Having a negative, distrustful attitude is detrimental to this process. Believing that you must "win" or you otherwise lose face is a bad attitude; in other words, feeling superior or feeling inferior are both problems. Try these actions to improve your conflict management and resolution abilities:

- ***Start by seeing those with whom you are in conflict as decent, reasonable persons who want to arrive at a fair solution.*** Deal with them with respect, just as you expect them to deal respectfully with you.

- Just as you would separate the person from his/her behavior, ***separate the person from the conflict the two of you are having.*** Start by clarifying to each other exactly what the conflict or problem involves. Find out what they want (i.e., their interests) and what they need (i.e., their position).  Ask for all the additional information you need to understand.  Don't try to offer solutions or "Mr. Fix-It" statements at this point.

- ***Recognize that there are probably many possible solutions that would meet both your interests and the other person's interests.***  Draw upon the things you both agree on and upon your shared goals and interests.  Draft some plans that will maximize the desired outcome for both of you.  Try to have several plans or ideas so that it doesn't appear as a "take-it-or-leave-it" proposition.

- ***Remember that both parties to a conflict are accountable for the outcome(s).***  Use "I" statements and avoid blaming "You" statements.  Coming to an agreement on the outcomes allows both parties to feel good about the process *and* the results.

Even if and when you develop a healthier approach to dealing with conflict in the workplace, it doesn't mean Chuck will!  Using the previous suggestions will help you navigate conflicts with the "Chucks" of the world.  Recognizing that Control Freaks often adopt competing strategies will allow you to respond more effectively to create more collaborative interactions.  And for conflict with Approval-holics who often compromise too quickly or avoid conflict all together, you will be more attuned to their fear of conflict and be able to help them see that respectful conflict is good for idea generation and creative solutions to problem-solving, not a means of disparaging or embarrassing people.

It is difficult to talk about extreme needs for control and approval without talking about the notion of perfectionism.  Interestingly, this challenge is found in both Control Freaks and Approval-holics, albeit for different reasons.  In the next chapter we look at those of you who struggle with a perfectionistic Chuck.

# CHAPTER 11

## The Challenge of Perfectionism

*"...le mieux est l'ennemi du bien." [translation: "...the perfect is the enemy of the good."]*
—Voltaire (1770)

### *Challenge #5: Being Overly Concerned with Being Perfect*

<u>What is a Perfectionist?</u>

Perfectionists are generally seen as people who desire social approval, yet they are also often controlling, demanding perfection not only from themselves, but also from others.[69] Those perfectionists who are in positions of power and influence and who are overly controlling cause conflict and stress for both those who work with them and for them.[70] Research has suggested that there are three types of perfectionists: self-oriented, other-oriented, and socially-prescribed.

---

[69] Flett, G.L., Hewitt, P.L., Blankstein, K.R., and Mosher, S.W. (1995). Perfectionism, life events, and depressive symptoms: A test of a diathesis-stress model. *Current Psychology*, 14, 112. doi:10.1007/BF02686885.

[70] Flett, G. L., & Hewitt, P. L. (2006). Perfectionism as a detrimental factor in leadership. *Inspiring leaders-2006*.

Extreme self-oriented perfectionists think about and strive for perfection, almost as a compulsion.[3] It isn't that they wish to be perfect, but that they *have* to be. They tend to be quite inflexible about how they approach tasks and relationships, even when the context suggests perfection is neither required nor possible, as described in this excerpt from a Leadership Development Plan:

> *When I work on a project, I can get so caught up in details that I will spend two to three times longer than I should be completing a task. I very often turn small jobs into very large ones by insisting on being so detailed in my work.*

Extreme self-oriented perfectionists are also likely to become addicted to work.

Other-oriented perfectionists demonstrate some hostility toward people who they feel are not approaching tasks, goals, behaviors, etc. as they should. They also may blame others for their own below-par performance and outcomes. In this way, other-oriented perfectionists could be considered to have an external locus of control (LOC), attributing their own failures to others who "messed them up."

Socially-prescribed perfectionists are hypersensitive to criticism and believe that others will value them only if they are perfect. This type of perfectionism has been found to be associated with depression and other mental health problems, including suicide and, as Flett and Hewitt note, "...can be particularly damaging for intimate relationships."[71]

As an example of a socially-prescribed perfectionist, Rachel Remen writes about a woman who was obsessed by her appearance.[72] She took such pains with how she appeared to others that she woke up thirty minutes before her husband did so as to be fully made up and dressed before he awoke. Though she loved her husband, she felt he lacked

[71] Flett, G.L., Hewitt, P.L.; Sherry, S.S. (2016). Deep, dark, and dysfunctional: The destructiveness of interpersonal perfectionism. Zeigler-Hill, Virgil (Ed); Marcus, David K. (Ed). *The dark side of personality: Science and practice in social, personality, and clinical psychology,* 211-229. Washington, DC, US: American Psychological Association, xi, 389 pp. http://dx.doi.org/10.1037/14854-011
[72] Remen, R.N. (1996). From "The long way home," *Kitchen Table Wisdom: Stories That Heal*, NY: Riverhead Books, pp. 110-113.

passion and spontaneity. In fact, he asked her permission every time before he kissed her.

But, one day, while she was trying on clothes in a department store, an earthquake struck, and she suddenly found herself out on the street, in the midst of glass, rubble, and water, dressed only in a very expensive dress and four-inch heels. All of her belongings—keys, purse, and money—were back in a dressing room inside the store that had collapsed. The woman walked eight hours to her home, and when she arrived shortly after midnight, she was dirty, sweaty, and disheveled. Her husband opened the door and, without a word, kicked the door closed and covered her dirty, tear-stained face with kisses. She had never met such an ardent response from her husband before, and when she asked him, he said simply, "I was always afraid of smearing your lipstick."

As Rachel Remen writes, "It is hard to trust someone with your vulnerability unless you can see in them a matching vulnerability and know that you will not be judged.

In some basic way it is our imperfections and even our pain that draws others close to us." The paradox with perfection is that the more perfect one attempts to be, the less perfect one's relationships with others become.

## Chuck the Perfectionist

Does your Chuck see events and experiences as good or bad, perfect or imperfect, black or white? In other words, there is no middle ground. Such thinking often leads to procrastination or abandonment of a task or project, because a requirement of flawless perfection, in even the smallest of tasks, can become fearfully overwhelming. If your Chuck is a perfectionist, does she believe that a flawless product or superb performance must be produced every time? In essence, one problem with perfectionists is that they believe that if it can't be done perfectly, it's not worth doing. Thus, a self-oriented perfectionist may spend so much time agonizing over some non-critical detail that a critical project misses its deadline or eventually, he or she just gives up on the project all together.

Additionally, if Chuck is an other-oriented perfectionist, he may be so compulsive that he may not tolerate other people's participation in a project or task. This is closely aligned with one's inability or fear of delegation, because one does not trust another person to have the same focus on perfection. That is, no one is as capable as the perfectionist of getting it "right." If tasks or project work are delegated and the outcome isn't "perfect," the perfectionist often shows hostility or superiority toward the person. In essence, though, this is just an attempt to shift the focus away from the perfectionist's own vulnerability and toward the other person's perceived inadequacy.

Remember that a perfectionist's focus can be on the final product of her work or the process of producing that product. In the first case, a relentless pursuit of the ultimate goal could be a good thing, but it ultimately becomes the perfectionist's greatest liability because of the overwhelming felt anxiety. It is this anxiety and foreboding that often sabotages their efforts.

Consider the case of a student who, at the beginning of every semester, puts every due date and every assignment for every class she is taking on her calendar. Rather than focusing on the assignments, projects, or tests that are due in the immediate future (a few days or weeks), she looks at the entire semester's work and feels totally overwhelmed and anxious! Ultimately, she may procrastinate beginning any of them, or she may work himself into a frenzy such that all her work suffers, primarily because she is so worried about doing every assignment perfectly.

In the second case, the perfectionist is more concerned with the processes involved in producing the outcome or achieving the goal. That is, he or she is primarily concerned with HOW something is done. These types of "Chucks" are equally likely to drive you crazy, because they get "in the weeds" of the details, making every step in a project as weighty as every other one.

The "perfect human" (and, by extension, the "perfect leader," "perfect employee," "perfect child," or "perfect spouse") is as appealing and mythical as the unicorn. Unfortunately, our organizations encourage striving for perfection. Like Ed Vargo, the major league baseball umpire, said about his work, "We're supposed to be perfect our first day on the job, and then show constant improvement."

Many of our greatest endeavors are indeed accomplished while striving to perfect ourselves. Great achievers, like perfectionists, want to improve; unlike perfectionists, they are willing to make mistakes and risk failure. Great achievers recognize mistakes, failure, and general imperfection as part of the reality of being human. Perfectionists, on the other hand, are trapped by the value they place on being "right" and having those around them recognize their worth.

In Robert Pirsig's well-known work, *Zen and the Art of Motorcycle Maintenance*, he relates the tale of the

"South Indian Monkey Trap." This gadget was developed by villagers to catch the numerous small monkeys inhabiting that part of the world. After placing rice inside a coconut chained to a stake, the villagers waited for the monkey to put his hand in a small hole in the coconut. The hole was big enough to stick his hand in it, but too small for his fist to come out after he had grabbed the rice. Tempted by the rice, the monkey reached in and was suddenly trapped. Not able to recognize that it was his own desire for the rice that trapped him, he was determined to hold onto the rice, because he wanted it. Unable to let go, he was trapped, and the villagers captured him.

Perfectionists need to rethink their own values and decide whether they are going to continue to be trapped by the emphasis they place on perfection or whether they can rid themselves of this obsession. Overcoming perfectionism requires courage, for it means accepting our own imperfections and humanness, as well as those of others. Like the other challenges discussed in this book, perfectionistic tendencies are driven by high needs for both approval and control.


## Identifying a Perfectionist "Chuck"

Dealing with *extreme* cases of perfectionism for yourself or your Chuck is beyond the scope of this book, as it generally requires intervention by a mental health professional. However, if your Chuck is a perfectionist, it would behoove you to decide if she is more of a self-oriented, other-oriented, or socially prescribed perfectionist. As you can likely identify by now, each type of perfectionism has some fundamental roots in both high needs for approval and control.

1. If your Chuck is more of a **self-oriented perfectionist**, she may

    • work an excessive number of hours and make sure her boss (and everyone else) is aware of the fact,

- compulsively re-do work (hers OR yours) that she believes isn't "perfect," thus wasting a lot of time in the process,

- think of performance or outcomes in dichotomous terms of either "success" or "failure,"

- avoid beginning projects or tasks if she cannot fully know the end result before she begins,

- actively display and proclaim her skills and successes (even taking credit for others' work), and

- do whatever it takes to achieve her goals, no matter what the cost.

2. If your Chuck is more of an **other-oriented perfectionist**, she may

- require direct reports or team members to work an excessive number of hours,

- ask direct reports and team members to re-do work that she doesn't think meets her high standards,

- have little empathy or regard for others and, in the extreme, may actually show hostility toward others who are held in high regard by co-workers,

customers, or leaders, and

- tend to blame others when projects do not come out

    as she expected.

3. If your Chuck is more of a **socially prescribed**

    **perfectionist**, she may

    - act differently in front of those whose regard is

        important to her and those whose regard isn't as

        important,

    - overreact to less-than-glowing feedback or criticism,

        redirecting the blame toward others,

    - have poor emotional control, lashing out at co-

        workers and direct reports or demonstrating

        inappropriate affect during conversations (e.g.,

        laughing at inappropriate times), and

    - create feelings of helplessness and hopelessness in

        others because of her impossibly high expectations.

Like all of Chuck's challenges you won't be able to

fundamentally change him or her; you can only adapt your own behavior and feelings. As with most everything we've discussed so far, because of his fragile self-esteem and need for approval and/or control, Chuck is keeping you at an emotional distance with his criticism and over-the-top demands. There are a few different strategies to deal with a perfectionist, and some of them are unique for dealing with boss "Chucks," and some are unique for dealing with direct report "Chucks."

## Dealing with a Perfectionist Boss

- If Chuck is harping on insignificant details, be respectful but honest. Tell him how it is affecting you and the project.

- If Chuck refuses to delegate work, tell him how important it is for you and your coworkers to learn and grow in your jobs and careers. Suggest several tasks that you feel you or others could handle.

- Discuss and try to nail down the specific priorities of the project together. For example, if Chuck is fixated on wordsmithing a sentence in a report, ask him to explain the consequences in relation to the rest of the content. In other words, is it worth the time to continue to work on it, given the amount of work left to do?

- Likewise, ask Chuck directly about his expectations. As a Control Freak, this may give him a feeling of control, and it minimizes (although it doesn't eliminate) the likelihood of criticism later.

- If Chuck is hypercritical, rather than get defensive, ask him what he would like you to do differently. This is much better strategy than challenging him on his criticism, because it puts the ball in his court to be specific about what he wants.

- Don't take Chuck's perfectionistic tendencies personally. Remind yourself that it is his problem, not you or your work, and that he sees his strive for perfection as a strength, not a weakness. It doesn't necessarily make it easier to work with him, but looking at it this way allows you to have a bit more patience with his neurosis.

- Above all, remind yourself that Chuck really does want to do his very best, and he wants you and your team to do your best, too. Viewed this way, it actually can be motivational.

## Dealing with a Perfectionist Direct Report

- Recognize that there are both positives and negatives to having a stickler on your team. Not everybody is geared to pay attention to the details, but perfectionists are.

- Explain the most annoying perfectionistic behaviors Chuck engages in to try to increase his self-awareness. He may not be aware that they drive you and others crazy! Saying something like, "I appreciate that you like to get everything right, but sometimes when you take time to redo work, it puts everybody else behind," allows Chuck to see the downside of his compulsion.

- Don't put Chuck in a role that is too complex. Perfectionists like jobs or tasks with very limited scope. Additionally, avoid placing Chuck in a role that requires him to manage people; otherwise, his demands for others' perfection will create bad feelings on the part of his direct reports.

- When giving Chuck feedback, ask how he would like to get it: "I would like to discuss your performance, but I'd like to know how you would like to proceed." It is also helpful to preface your discussion by asking him, "Is there anything in your last assignment that you wish you had done differently (or better)?"

- Remember that perfectionists won't be able to change unless they want to, so refrain from nagging them.

## Working on Your Own Perfectionism

If you have a tendency toward perfectionism yourself, here are several strategies that will help you recognize and replace perfectionist behavior with more achievement-focused behavior:

- *Increase your awareness of the self-critical nature of your "all-or-nothing" thoughts.* When you find yourself berating a less-than-perfect performance, whether yours or someone else's, force yourself to look at and acknowledge the good parts of that performance. Ask yourself, "Is it really as bad as I feel it is?" and "How do other people really see it?"

- *Analyze how your perfectionism relates to other problems or situations in your life.* Like with the automatic thought analysis earlier, you can look at other aspects of your life with the same eye as you do your work performance. You may discover that problems with significant relationships, excessive workaholism, eating and substance

abuse problems, other compulsive behaviors,

anxiety, nervousness, feelings of inadequacy, self-

criticism, etc. can be attributed to your

compulsion about having perfect outcomes.

When you begin by asking the question, "In what

other areas do I require perfection?" you may

begin to note a pattern across all spheres of your

life.

- ***Set realistic goals.*** By setting more achievable

and realistic goals, you will gradually realize that

"imperfect" results do not lead to the punitive

consequences you expect and fear. For example,

suppose you swim laps every day for relaxation

and exercise. You set a goal of 20 laps, but you

can barely swim 10 laps. In your old

"perfectionist" mode, you would soon feel

disappointed at your poor performance and

anxious about improving it. You may even give

up swimming because you're not "good enough."
But if you tell yourself that 10 laps are good
enough for now, and you set a realistic goal of
adding one lap each week, you continue
swimming without anxiety. You don't necessarily
stop trying to improve, but you swim for fun and
exercise. That is one huge drawback to
perfectionists: they often miss out on fun!

- ***Set strict time limits on each of your projects.***
  When the time is up, move on, and attend to
  another activity. This will help reduce the
  procrastination that typically results from
  perfectionism. Suppose you must do research for
  a report and presentation that is due in two days.
  Decide that you will spend only three hours
  looking up the research facts you need, three more
  hours writing the report, and two hours preparing
  the slides and your talk. If you stick to your time
  limits, you won't spend the entire time searching

for elusive information, and then feel rushed to write and prepare the entire report and presentation.

- ***Practice leaving something undone.*** Perfectionists may find this hard to believe, but not everything is equally important, nor are there equal expectations about every behavior and outcome in our lives! For example, sometimes it is more important to leave the dishes undone after dinner so that you can spend time with a child whose best friend just moved away. Likewise, at work, not everything has "top priority." Practice intentionally leaving one thing undone every day, even if you could complete it. It will help you to realize that there are not equal consequences for all behaviors and outcomes.

- ***Learn how to deal with criticism.*** Perfectionists often view criticism as a personal attack, and then they respond defensively. Concentrate on being more objective about the criticism and about yourself. If someone criticizes you for making a mistake, acknowledge the mistake and assert your right to make mistakes. Remind yourself that if you stop making mistakes, you also stop learning and growing. Once you no longer buy into the fallacy that humans must be perfect to be worthwhile, you won't feel so angry or defensive when you make a mistake. Criticism will then seem like a natural thing from which to learn, rather than something to be avoided at all costs.

- *Ask yourself how important this will be in a year.* When we look at our performance mistakes, we often are right in the middle of the issue. We forget that "this, too, shall pass." When you are unsatisfied with your behavior or performance outcome, asking "how important will this really be to my future?" can help you put the event in its proper perspective.

- ***Reward yourself for what you do get done, and don't punish yourself (or others) for what doesn't get done.*** Perfectionists are often those who see the glass half-empty, rather than half-full. Begin by looking at what was accomplished and provide reinforcement for what was done and done correctly. Work at focusing on your accomplishments rather than your perceived failures.

Most perfectionists struggle with both outcome and process, as well as with people who they perceive are not as committed, talented, or motivated as they are. As a result, the perfectionistic Chucks of the world also likely struggle with making decisions. That challenge is one that is particularly problematic for leaders and managers, as we will see in the next chapter.

# CHAPTER 12

## The Challenge of Indecision

*The greatest mistake you can make in life is to be continually fearing you will make one.*
   —Elbert Hubbard, U.S. author (1856-1915)

### Challenge #6: Inability or Unwillingness to Make Decisions

The final challenge we will discuss involves an inability or unwillingness to make decisions. This challenge manifests itself in different ways, but primarily it is experienced as indecision or anxiety about making a decision due to an underlying fear of making a mistake. Sometimes fear of decision-making significantly impacts our quality of life by causing panic attacks or keeping us apart from others. It can even turn into an actual phobia called *decidophobia*, the fear of making your own decisions. But, as Daft and Lengel point out, "the fear of failure is worse than the failure itself."[73]  What lies at the heart of this challenge is a need to avoid disapproval from others or a desire to avoid repeating poor decisions.

Clearly, most of our daily decisions are not earth-shattering, but you can imagine how paralysis in the decision-making process would render us virtually incapacitated every day if we let it.  We are called upon to be courageous, reliable, and trustworthy with regard to the *outcome* of our decisions (i.e., to make decisions consistent with our core values and beliefs).  In addition, we are also called upon to engage in a transparent and consistent decision-making *process* (i.e., to clarify for others how we make decisions and the logic of our decision-making).

According to Susan Jeffers, author of *Feel the Fear and Do It Anyway*, when fear or anxiety crop up during your decision-making, the fear is based either on your belief that you won't be able to handle the outcome of your decision or on your doubts about whether you have enough correct

[73] Daft, R.L. and Lengel, R.H. (2000).  *Fusion Leadership*, San Francisco, CA: Berrett-Koehler Publishers, Inc., p. 162.

information to make the best decision.[74] Thus, our indecision may lie in our fears and doubts about the outcomes of our decisions or about the process of decision-making:

*The burdens that make us groan and sweat,*

*The troubles that make us fume and fret,*

*Are the things that haven't happened yet.*

–George W. Bain

## Fear of Poor Decision Outcomes

Ever hear the story about the frog that fell into a deep rut in the road and, try as he might, he could not get out? Mrs. Frog, standing above the rut, admonished, cajoled, beckoned, and belittled him to no avail.

"Get out, come on, let's go," she pleaded.

But Mr. Frog, down in the deep rut, said simply, "There is no way I can get out of this rut."

---

[74] Jeffers, S. (1987). *Feel the Fear and Do It Anyway*, New York: Ballantine Books.

Leaving him there, Mrs. Frog hopped down to the pond and, in a few minutes, Mr. Frog appeared beside her on their favorite lily pad.

"I thought you said you couldn't get out," she exclaimed.

He responded, "A big truck came along, and I had to."

Sometimes our fears paralyze us to the point that we cannot decide anything. This is represented by the philosophical concept referred to as "Buridan's Ass," which states that, given the option of two equally wonderful piles of hay, the ass will starve to death, because it cannot choose.

Sometimes we resign ourselves to the fact that we will never be able to do, or be, or have whatever it is we need or want. And sometimes, like Mr. Frog, we are forced to make a decision, whether it is the one we want to make or not. We let other people or our circumstances dictate our decisions, rather than depending upon our inner voice to help us.

So, how do we handle these fears and avoid these behaviors?

## The Role of Procrastination

Consider how someone who is fearful about the outcome of a decision might behave. First, he or she may procrastinate, putting off the decision and avoiding the outcome all together. Procrastination is a major symptom of one's inability to make a decision. In his research on procrastination, Neil Fiore found that

> We procrastinate when we fear a threat to our sense of worth and independence. We only act lazy when our natural drive for fruitful activity is threatened or suppressed. The deep inner fears that cause us to seek such unproductive forms of relief are suggested to be the fear of failure, the fear of being imperfect, perfectionism, and the fear of impossible expectations, of being overwhelmed. These fears prevent us from working on and attaining possible goals and relationships. [75]

[75] Fiore, N.A. (1989). *The Now Habit*. New York: Tarcher/Putnam, division of Penguin Putnam, Inc.

Procrastination is a means of escape from reality. The person who procrastinates is like the person who avoids conflict, i.e., "If I don't deal with the issue or problem, it will go away." But rarely does a problem just disappear, particularly problems that real people and real organizations face. More often than not, problems increase in scope, depth, or impact as time passes and we put off the decision.

Solving procrastination is really a matter of analyzing what the predominant fear is about making a decision. For example, for those of you who have a high need for approval, you can reduce your fear of failing by seeing that your worth is not totally determined by the outcome of any one particular decision. For those of us who have a high need for control, the fear lies in letting go of the decision-making process or losing control over the outcome of a decision.

Keeping a record of the circumstances surrounding your avoidance of making a decision, noting such things as what excuses were used and what your thoughts and feelings were about the decision or decision process, will place the focus on whether your fears are real or imagined. Such analysis will help reduce your tendency to procrastinate, but it may not completely solve the problem. You have to actually stop procrastinating! Like the poem goes,

*Procrastination is my sin,*

*It brings me endless sorrow,*

*I really must stop doing it.*

*In fact...I'll stop tomorrow.*

## The Impossibility of an "Optimal" Choice

In addition to procrastination, a person may also over value the importance of the outcome of a decision and react by vacillating between choices. The more important that you perceive the outcome to be, the more likely you will be to evaluate in detail all of the available choices. The problem is that we get hung up in deciding on the "best" outcome. We try to find all the information and data to help us to know, for sure, what we should do so that we don't make a poor decision.

None of us knows enough to avoid making some mistakes. Likewise, none of us could possibly gather all the information necessary to know everything before we make a decision. In fact, recent scientific evidence suggests that the more information and time we have to make a decision, the less likely we are to make a good one.[76]

We often get so overwhelmed with information that we become paralyzed among all the choices, like the mother who took her three children into a small ice cream parlor for an ice cream cone. The man behind the counter asked, "Chocolate or vanilla?" The mother asked him, "Why don't you have more flavors?" "Lady," he answered, "if you only knew how much time it takes some people to make up their minds between chocolate and vanilla, you wouldn't ask that!"

Herbert A. Simon, 1978 Nobel Prize winner for his work on decision-making and cognition, coined the term *satisficing* to explain why we can never know enough to

---

[76] Dijksterhuis, A., Bos, W., Nordgren, L.F., and van Baaren, R.B. (2006). *On Making the Right Choice: The Deliberation-Without-Attention Effect*, 311, 5763, pp. 1005 – 1007.

make the optimal decision. He reasoned that we can never achieve the optimal or best alternative, primarily because we are limited by not knowing the total consequences of our decisions. He termed this limitation *bounded rationality*. Since we can't know everything before we are asked to decide and, therefore, cannot choose the best alternative among every possible one, we have to be content with an alternative that meets some, but perhaps not all, of our criteria.

For example, let us imagine that your car has just died and you need another one. Before you get another car, you make a list of what you must have in a car, e.g., four doors, automatic transmission, blue exterior, CD player, and automatic windows. You also determine that you cannot afford a brand new car and, therefore, will need to purchase one that is at least two years old.

At this point, how do you decide which car you should purchase? You can never evaluate every two-year-old (or older) car with your stated attributes; it would be impossible to locate them all. So, you begin to look at the available options within a "bounded" rationale. In other words, you restrict your options to geographic area, price point, time commitment, etc. At some point, you will be faced with several alternatives that meet your specifications. But you will never know if the car you ultimately choose is the *best* car—only whether or not the car is a satisfactory choice in that it meets all the criteria you said you must have. That's *satisficing*!

If You Report to an Indecisive Chuck

As Vineet Nayar writes, "bad bosses can deflate the best intentions, disable the most enthusiastic people, and freeze the hottest ideas."[77] If you work for an indecisive Chuck, there are a few simple ways to work through indecision:

---

[77] Nayar, V. (2014). Managing 3 types of bad bosses, *Harvard Business Review,* December 1. Retrieved from https://hbr.org/2014/12/managing-3-types-of-bad-bosses, February 6, 2017.

- *Help Chuck define the problem or the question.* One way to do this is to ask questions about the goal or outcome Chuck is seeking. By helping work toward a specific target for the decision it may help limit the range of alternatives and, subsequently, make a decision more manageable.

- *Talk to people in different roles or departments.* No one has a monopoly on the right answer. In many cases, talking to others across the organization who have experience in the problem or a stake in the outcome of the decision may offer different perspectives on it than what you or Chuck have at the moment.

- *Ask Chuck for a timeframe for a decision to be made that is BEFORE the deadline it is due.* Making decisions at the last possible minute is a typical behavior of an indecisive person. Chuck may postpone decisions because of anxiety about making the wrong one or because of being paralyzed by too many alternatives or too much analysis. In either case, waiting until the last minute forgoes the opportunity to refine a poor decision. The earlier the decision is made, the more time there is to change it if the initial actions indicate it is not correct.

- ***Beg for forgiveness, rather than ask for permission.*** Sometimes it is better to act than not to act, particularly if the goal is clear and the alternatives are relatively straightforward. Indecisive Chucks often prefer someone else to take the reins, because then they don't have accountability for the outcomes. It sounds counterintuitive, but if your Chuck has a high need for approval, it allows him to say after a decision was made, "I really had nothing to do with this decision." Of course, if the decision ends up being a good one, Chucks with a high need for control will likely take the credit for it!

## If an Indecisive Chuck Reports to You

Many of your subordinates have high approval or control needs and also demonstrate indecision. That is where you, as their boss, need to establish a culture of decisiveness by coaching and encouraging your direct reports who are perhaps afraid of making the wrong decision (thereby risking your disapproval).     In order to encourage Chuck to make a decision and act on it, here are some ideas to try:

- ***Make sure you are open to hearing alternatives from Chuck.*** Being open means asking questions. Asking "What haven't we thought of yet?" give permission for subordinates to express their views.

- ***Express yourself candidly, but respectfully.*** One of the hallmarks of combating indecisiveness is to say honestly what you see and hear, but in a spirit of dialogue, not a soapbox diatribe. The word, *candor* or *candid*, comes from the Latin word, *candēre*, meaning "to shine." In this case, being candid with your Chuck will encourage him to shine, i.e., to be authentically himself.

- ***Remember that indecision is ultimately a behavioral issue, not a cognitive one.*** Although your Chuck may seem to be mulling over alternatives or fiddling with the process, he may just be immobilized by fear. Even when Chuck has committed to a decision, he may procrastinate acting on it. This is still indecision! If this happens, don't revisit the decision; rather, hold him accountable for the procrastination. Resurrecting the decision itself allows Chuck to go back to contemplation, reanalysis, and stalling. Remind him that the decision has already been made and that now you are expecting him to act.

- ***Provide appropriate feedback to Chuck on the process and outcome of his decision.*** If the decision and subsequent action on it turns out positively, praise Chuck. If it turns out negatively, sit down and have an open, candid discussion. Asking questions, such as "Where do you think we went wrong here?" gives him permission to re-evaluate and learn from a poor decision process or outcome. Such an approach also sends an important message from his boss (you):

"Not every decision will turn out the way we want it
to, and that's OK. The most important thing is what
we learn from them." The U.S. Army's approach,
called an "After-Action Review (AAR),"[78] is a good
example of how to do this.

Chronic indecision can be one of the toughest
challenges for any of us. It is so difficult because it goes to
the very heart of our needs for approval and control. We
don't want people to think we're dumb, and we don't want to
give up our control over what we consider "important"
decisions. But there is a fine line between being judicious
and being paralyzed with indecision. The judicious decision-
maker recognizes that they want the best information and
data they can get, but realize that, at some point, a decision
has to be made and acted upon. But it is the fear of losing
approval from others and/or losing control over the process

---

[78] A Leader's Guide to After-Action Reviews, Headquarters, Department
of the Army, September 1993. Retrieved from
http://www.au.af.mil/au/awc/awcgate/army/tc_25-20/tc25-20.pdf (public
domain).

or the outcome that often prevents us from actually making a decision.

## Working on Your Own Indecision

If you are someone for whom indecision is a challenge, here are some very practical suggestions to help you deal with your fears and doubts about making decisions.

- *Become more aware of the fears that underlie your indecisiveness.* Keep a journal of decisions that you struggled with and analyze why you struggled with them. Or write down what you are afraid of as you begin the decision-making process, noting if any of the reasons have an approval or control basis. This will help bring those fears out into the open so that you can begin to question their validity.

- *Set some specific and realistic criteria for your decision.* Doing this ahead of time will prevent you from vacillating after you've determined all the alternatives. You'll remember in our car purchase example the color, number of doors, transmission type, etc. was determined *before* starting to look at options. This makes evaluation of your choice easier in the end, since anything that doesn't meet the criteria is not a viable option.

- *Ask for others' input for options or alternatives.* Most of the time, your fears and anxieties occur when a decision rests on you. Although you may be making the ultimate decision, sometimes it is helpful to get other people's ideas about alternatives you might consider. This doesn't mean you have to adopt their ideas; it merely means you are in an information-and-opinion-gathering mode. It is your choice to include their ideas or not. But it usually doesn't cost anything to ask, and they may give some great information or ideas that may never have occurred to you!

- *Accept the concept of "bounded rationality."* If you continually search for more and better data, you will never make a decision.  Set limits on how much time and effort you will expend on a particular decision, and stick to those limits.

- ***Broaden your experiences***.  This is probably the single most helpful effort in making good decisions. By exposing yourself to a variety of different experiences, you are able to look at things from different perspectives.  For example, consider spending some time in another culture, country, or even in another part of town if you live in a large, urban area.  This experience puts your immediate concerns into their proper perspective.  It can also provide alternative ways to see problems and issues, comparing them to seemingly unrelated situations, and offer new opportunities and alternatives.

Of course, you could always approach decision-making as the Persians did in 450 B.C., as recounted by Herodotus in *The Histories*, although it may not go over well in your workplace!

*If an important decision is to be made [the Persians] discuss the question when they are drunk... the following day, the master of the house...submits their decision for reconsideration when they are sober. If they still approve it, it is adopted; if not, it is abandoned. Conversely, any decision they make when they are sober is reconsidered afterwards when they are drunk.*

## What's Next?

In the last several chapters we have identified six primary challenges that Chucks (as well as many of us) struggle with in both our personal and professional lives. Although you may not be challenged by all of them, it is likely that most of you reading this book have at least one or two challenges that have been holding you back from being as successful as you could become. And, of course, you have "Chucks" at work who drive you crazy with some of their behaviors around these challenges.

Understanding how high needs for approval and control influence why we have these challenges will help you to choose ways to minimize their impact on your work relationships. And, if your "Chuck" has some of these challenges, hopefully you now have a few more effective strategies to deal with him or her!

In the concluding chapter we will talk about using what you have learned about needs for control and approval to give the Chucks in your life, as well as yourself, some grace and space. Because, if we do, it is less likely that Control Freaks and Approval-holics will drive us CRAZY!

# CHAPTER 13

## Grace Notes: Changing Your Experience with Chuck

*You can often change your circumstances by changing your attitude.*

–Eleanor Roosevelt

As you've no doubt experienced, the "Chucks" of your work lives, whether they are bosses, peers, or direct reports, demonstrate a number of irritating behaviors that are based, to a large degree, on how controlling or approval-seeking they are. Along the way you've hopefully learned a few techniques for dealing more professionally with these Control Freaks and Approval-holics, i.e., the "People Who Drive You CRAZY at Work."

But merely demonstrating good behavioral techniques in the face of challenges like poor conflict management, unwillingness to delegate, perfectionism, inability to make a decision, impatience, anger, and generally poor interpersonal skills will not change the essence of a "Chuck." In fact, probably nothing you can do will fundamentally change him or her. Nevertheless, in addition to the strategies outlined in the previous chapters, you also now have more insight into why Chuck drives you crazy, so that you can choose how to respond, rather than merely react in the moment.

The ability to step outside of ourselves to look at the situation more objectively helps us to develop our self-awareness, as well as to assess the situation so that we are able to give people some room to be who they are. It doesn't mean we don't hold them accountable for their actions but, at the very least, their behavior doesn't have to drive us crazy, either. The key is in how we acknowledge who they are— and who we are—and apply a few *grace notes*.

## What Do Grace Notes Have to Do with Chuck?

In music, grace notes are musical "ornaments" that are added to a melody to delay very slightly the appearance of a principal note. In essence, when attached to a principal note, a grace note reduces the time value of the principal note; for example, it may cut the time of a quarter note in half. Although the principal quarter note is still played, it doesn't last as long with a grace note attached to it as it would without one.

**Figure 2. An appoggiatura grace note attached to a quarter note**

One example of a frequently used grace note is an *appoggiatura*, which comes from the Italian verb, *appoggiare*, which means "to lean upon." *Appoggiaturas* are not required by the principal note, nor do they detract from the original music's structure, i.e., the story told by the music. But the added ornament of an *appoggiatura* to a principal note is able to change the listener's experience of the music in both subtle and profound ways. They are generally played or sung with a lighter touch. A grace note is not meant to be consciously heard, but to support or "lean upon" and embellish the principal note. As such, grace notes are a means of providing some freedom for personal expression, while enhancing the experience—even changing it—for the performer and the listener.

So what do grace notes have to do with your interactions with Chuck?

In dealing with the Chucks of our lives, we can add a "grace note" to Chuck's behaviors by recognizing that we all need someone to "lean upon" at times, reminding us that we each have irritating behaviors that drive some people crazy. In other words, with regard to control and approval, if we can remember that all of us have some controlling and some approval-seeking behaviors, we will be able to more readily understand why Chucks behave the way they do, and realize that we, too, are likely to be a "Chuck" in someone else's life. By doing some very intentional listening and forgiveness beneath the actual words or actions, we not only give our Chuck the ability to be who he is, but we are also able to change our own experience and attitude toward him. Let's look at a real-life example of someone we all are familiar with to provide insight on how we might do this.

## Abraham Lincoln and His Team of Rivals

Doris Kearns Goodwin, in her acclaimed book, *Team of Rivals*, outlines the unprecedented decision Lincoln made to bring his most vocal critics and presidential rivals into his cabinet. Among several others, William Seward was appointed as Secretary of State; Salmon P. Chase accepted the post of Secretary of the Treasury; Edward Bates became the Attorney General. Interestingly, these rivals of Lincoln had some traits that were similar to each other:

- All were lawyers.
- All were ambitious.
- All were egotistical and strong-minded.
- All were better educated than Abraham Lincoln.
- All wanted power.

Moreover, each of these men had a very low opinion of Lincoln before, and even shortly after, he became President. In essence, each acted as a "Chuck" to Abraham Lincoln.

Seward was particularly dubious about Lincoln's political acumen, and tried to sabotage his presidency. Chase thought himself to be a better leader than Lincoln, and during his tenure as Secretary of the Treasury, he tendered his resignation three times in order to force Lincoln's hand to appoint particular people to roles in the administration. Bates did not always support Lincoln's policies and was vocal in voicing his dissent to them, particularly the Emancipation Proclamation and the recruitment of black soldiers into the Union army. These competitors and rivals, however, became his biggest supporters and allies throughout his abbreviated term as President of the United States of America.

So how did Abraham Lincoln use "grace notes" to turn powerful competitors who initially thought him weak and incompetent into friends, confidantes, and allies? Kearns Goodwin describes it like this:

*....through his [Lincoln's] extraordinary array of personal qualities that enabled him to form friendships with men who had previously opposed him; to repair injured feelings that, left untended, might have escalated into permanent hostility; to assume responsibility for the failures of subordinates; to share credit with ease; and to learn from mistakes.*[79]

Doris Kearns Goodwin further describes that his personality and life experiences also played a central role in changing his relationships with his rivals:

*Lincoln's abhorrence of hurting another was born of a more than simple compassion. He possessed extraordinary empathy – the gift or curse of putting himself in the place of another, to experience what they were feeling, to understand their motives and desires.*[80] *...his years of travel on the circuit through central Illinois, engaging people in taverns, on street corners, and in shops, [during which] Lincoln had*

---

[79] Kearns Goodwin, D. (2005). *Team of Rivals*. New York: Simon & Schuster, p. xvii.
[80] Kearns Goodwin, D. (2005). *Team of Rivals*. New York: Simon & Schuster, p. 104

*developed a keen sense of what people felt, thought,*
*needed, and wanted.*[81]

Lincoln's rivals were changed by their experiences with him, partially because of his ability to empathize and understand what was driving their behaviors. We can use similar approaches to help us deal with our Chucks. Part of becoming a grace note for Chuck is to begin with the notion of "holding space."

## Holding Space for Chuck

It is often in the immediate interactions that we need to "hold space" for Chuck. "Holding space" really means to be mindful and to focus on what is going on at the moment—emotions, body language, and words—without becoming reactive. It reminds us that when we react negatively to someone, or when we think we know how to advise them, we are, in fact, taking their power away from them—a basic

---

[81] Kearns Goodwin, D. (2005). *Team of Rivals*. New York: Simon & Schuster, p. 255.

determinant of the behaviors for those who have high needs for control and approval.

"Holding space" also allows people to make different decisions and to have different experiences than us. It is about respecting each person's differences and recognizing that those differences may lead to them making choices that we would not make. When we hold space, we release control and honor differences.

"Holding space" involves knowing when to give advice and when to withhold it. Recognizing the areas in which they feel most vulnerable and incapable and offering the right kind of help without shaming them takes practice and humility. This is particularly true if you are in a position to give a performance evaluation or provide feedback and coaching to a Chuck.

One challenge for all of us who have to deal with a Chuck is to recognize that we, too, are likely to be a Chuck in someone else's life. As such, we need to understand how our reaction to Chuck is driven by, and is a reflection of, our own needs for control and approval. For example, if we have a high need for control, we may be more likely to be driven crazy by Chuck's seemingly endless paralysis in decision-making. If we have a high need for approval, we may see Chuck's unwillingness to delegate work to us as a personal rejection. Likewise, if we work for or with a Chuck who is more similar to us, we tend to be more tolerant and understanding. The better we are at accepting ourselves and our Chucks, the more compassionate and empathetic we become.

## Learning Chuck's "Story"

To understand someone well is to know her story—the experiences that have shaped her, the trials and turning points that have tested her. Before we can achieve a measure of compassion and empathy for Chuck, we must understand her story or, more specifically, what the underlying triggers are that prompt the behaviors that drive us crazy. Remember that these behaviors are often triggered by anxiety, so learning what triggers Chuck's anxiety will help you to not only know when the approval-seeking or controlling behaviors will appear, but also give you some insight on things you can do to help him or her avoid the triggering event(s) or, at least, better understand the anxiety caused by the triggering event(s). Here's a personal example to show you what I mean.

My wife is a minister. On at least three occasions when we have left on a two-week vacation, a disruptive event in her church has occurred while she's been gone. These events have caused some congregational division or a personal grievance that made our time away stressful and anxiety-ridden. As a result, any time she is scheduled to be away for a period of time, she experiences some angst before she goes and while she is gone.

In this example, the triggering event is "being away from the church"; her previous unpleasant experiences cause anxiety, which result in her increased need for control over what goes on during the period of time she's gone (e.g., leaving detailed instructions, frequent checking in with staff). Without knowing the back story, her current staff would likely wonder why she is behaving in such a controlling way right before vacation. But by knowing what she has experienced in the past while on vacation, they can be much more compassionate and understanding, knowing WHY they need detailed instructions on seemingly unlikely events or WHEN to provide her with frequent updates on what is going on back home.

## The Paradox of Dealing with Chuck

Our tendency is to distance ourselves from someone who is overly controlling or approval-seeking. But, the paradox is that *in order to learn Chuck's story, we must spend more time with him to get to know him better.* This type of "knowing" means taking a genuine interest in the person, separate from his work performance and annoying behavior. Some of you might be thinking, "But how do I do that in the workplace without appearing to be prying or asking personal and inappropriate questions of a colleague, direct report, or boss?" There are several approaches that work quite well and that are professionally appropriate:

- <u>Engage in team building exercises</u>. While many of us have been through some of these and may have thought them stupid or trivial, there are some benefits if the exercise is chosen well and has a relevance to discovering triggering events. One example is to ask a group to share where they grew up and their birth order among siblings, as well as a question about a unique or interesting challenge from their childhood.[82] These questions can point to where their control or approval needs may have originally arisen (since they usually begin early in life). Of course, it is important to make a safe space for sharing and to instruct people that they don't have to share anything they don't want to. You may be surprised, however, at what they do share with each other and with

---

[82] This exercise is similar to one found in Patrick Lencioni's book, *Overcoming the five dysfunctions of a team: Field guide for leaders, managers and facilitators.*

you. As a result, you'll be more attuned to triggers in the workplace that might be a control or approval challenge for them.

- Ask about "highs" and "lows": Every person has things that happen that are both positive and negative. Allowing people to share both the exciting things that are happening in their lives, as well as the things for which they need affirmation or support, provides you with insight into those things that can trigger anxiety and those that can help them get through tough times.

- Self-disclosure. One of the best ways to get someone to share insight into their behavior is for you to share your own story. This doesn't mean airing dirty laundry or grievances. Rather, it is the art of taking an incremental approach to letting someone know and, hopefully, understand your own experiences, both successes and challenges. Of course, we have to walk a fine line when it comes to self-disclosure. Skillful self-disclosers choose the substance and process of their revelations, including the depth, breadth, and timing of disclosure, with the goal of furthering trustworthiness and cooperation, rather than furthering personal agendas. Consider the example of a chief nursing officer who was charged with developing a cost-savings reorganization plan at her hospital. At a staff meeting, she was met by anger and anxiety from employees who were concerned about potential job losses. By self-disclosing that she, herself, had been downsized early in her career and sharing her vision of a reorganization that would cut costs, not people (and, thus, sparing the employees from her own previous experience), she was able to gain trust from staff members that she would work with them to come up with a reorganization plan.

## Concluding Thoughts

The ability to offer some space and grace is the hallmark of successfully dealing with your Chuck and saving yourself a lot of anger, anxiety, and grief, even if you think they don't deserve it. I think Frederick Buechner said it best: *Grace is something you can never get but only be given. There's no way to earn it or deserve it or bring it*

*about any more than you can deserve the taste of raspberries*

*and cream or earn good looks or bring about your own*

*birth.*[83]

Because the "Chucks" of our workplaces and our

lives have stories that we don't usually take time to learn, we

tend to react to their behaviors with our reptilian brains,

rather than with our rational brains.  By using some of the

suggestions presented throughout the book, over time you

will get better at dealing with your Chuck.  Moreover, by

trying to understand what triggers their behaviors and then,

with a knowing little smile, intentionally decide to offer them

grace, you will be in a much better frame of mind and, I

suspect, so will your Chuck.

[83] Buechner, F. (1993). *Wishful thinking: A seeker's ABC*. New York: HarperOne.

## About the Author

Dr. Dale J. Dwyer joined The University of Toledo faculty in 1989 and is Professor of Management and former Chair of the Department of Management. He holds a Ph.D. in Business Administration from the University of Nebraska-Lincoln, and both an M.A. and B.A. in Communication from the University of Cincinnati.

Dr. Dwyer is an award-winning teacher and the author of the top-selling SHRM-published book, *Got a Minute? The 9 Lessons Every HR Professional Must Learn* (2010). His other books include, *Got A Solution? HR Approaches to 5 Common and Persistent Business Problems* (2014) and *Needy People: Working Successfully with Control Freaks and Approval-holics.*"

Dr. Dwyer consults with both for-profit and not-for-profit organizations on human resource management and leadership development projects. His research is primarily in the areas of employee control and stress, and he holds board membership and offices with several professional societies and community boards.

**New Book Coming in January 2019!**

*Managing in a 21$^{st}$ Century Organization*
**ISBN: 9781524965884**

**Kendall Hunt Publishing**
**https://www.kendallhunt.com/**

Made in the USA
Columbia, SC
15 July 2019